IN THE INTERLUDE

BORIS PASTERNAK

IN THE
INTERLUDE

POEMS

1945-1960

*Translated into English Verse
by Henry Kamen*

*With a Foreword by
Sir Maurice Bowra
and Notes by
George Katkov*

LONDON
OXFORD UNIVERSITY PRESS
NEW YORK   TORONTO
1962

Oxford University Press, Amen House, London E.C.4

GLASGOW NEW YORK TORONTO MELBOURNE WELLINGTON
BOMBAY CALCUTTA MADRAS KARACHI LAHORE DACCA
CAPE TOWN SALISBURY NAIROBI IBADAN ACCRA
KUALA LUMPUR HONG KONG

*First published in this edition with facing Russian
text,* 1962, *with simultaneous publication
of the translations only in
Oxford Paperbacks*

891.71
P

The translator and publisher acknowledge the permission of
Messrs. William Collins Sons and Co. Ltd. for the right to
publish extracts from their translation of *Dr. Zhivago* and *An
Essay in Autobiography* by Boris Pasternak and for the right to
publish a new translation of the poems in *Dr. Zhivago*.

PRINTED IN GREAT BRITAIN
BY BILLING & SONS LIMITED, GUILDFORD AND LONDON

To Karen, who helped:

Ты — благо гибельного шага,
Когда житье тошней недуга,
А корень красоты — отвага,
И это тянет нас друг к другу.

FOREWORD

In the last thirty years of his life Boris Pasternak published almost no original poetry. Apart from two or three slim volumes, not of the highest quality, issued during the war, his public output was limited to his noble translations of Shakespeare and Goethe. If asked about him, orthodox Russian writers would speak disparagingly of him as 'the translator', as if they had never heard of his poetry. In this they displayed the dishonesty of their kind; for Pasternak's earlier poems were widely quoted in many circles, and when the authorities stopped the further publication of original poems by him, they no doubt feared that this unpolitical and independent man, with his passionate convictions about the integrity of art, would by his example discredit official theories of what art ought to be. None the less in these years of apparent silence Pasternak did not abandon poetry. If much of his time was given to translation and to *Dr. Zhivago*, these were incentives to turn his poetical gifts in new directions and to find at last for his genius that full scope in which he had so long been hindered by the literary policies, at once gruesome and grotesque, of the Soviet Union. Just because he had no hope of publishing any more poetry, he could say with the utmost candour what otherwise he might have had to disguise or distort, and he could apply to this his ripe, matured notions of what poetry ought to be. He wrote now for himself and for posterity, but not for any immediate recognition or renown. The hard restrictions to which the authorities subjected him had a notable effect on his art.

Pasternak himself was fully conscious of this. He felt that these later poems were much better than any he had written hitherto, and it was by them that he wished to be remembered. In this he was unjust to his earlier work which, at least in his brilliant years between 1919 and 1922, had a most unusual vitality and brilliance. But a poet may well turn against his earlier work if he is obsessed by a desire to write differently, and this Pasternak certainly was. As his faith in the Russian Revolution waned through the long tyranny of Stalin, he turned in on himself and searched his heart for what mattered most in his life, and he found that his new subjects called for a new manner, less brilliant and less experimental than of old, but more solidly based in human nature and more truly expressive of his graver, quieter moods. He transformed his style not so obviously as Yeats did in the years after 1910 but certainly with an equal increase in power and depth and humanity. The old shocks and surprises and paradoxes have been eliminated; the movement of the verse is much more regular; the experiences presented with such sincerity and self-knowledge are closer to those of other men. The language, which in its day had learned so much from Mayakovsky, has been brought closer to modern speech, not merely in the order and choice of its words but even in the rhythm of its lines. Yet this simplification has not impaired but increased the old power, which is still present everywhere but in closer control and held more in reserve.

To translate these poems calls for a high degree of sensibility, technique, and knowledge. Mr. Kamen would not claim that his translations are perfect, since after all no translations ever are or can hope to be. But he understands Pasternak's spirit from the inside with an intuitive sympathy, and his command of English verse is such that in it he comes very close to Pasternak's own precise and exacting form. Pasternak remained throughout his creative career a classical writer in the sense that he could work best through a strict discipline, and that is why he never followed the Futurists in their rejection of regular stanzas and rhymes. His choice of rhymes is always highly original and ingenious, but it is not disturbing; the regular progress of his stanzas emphasizes both the strength and the self-control of his emotions. It is this classical quality that Mr. Kamen's translation catches. It is possible to translate Pasternak in other ways, to pay no attention to his form and to concentrate on the echoes and associations evoked by his words, but this is not necessarily the best way, and it is not the way in which Pasternak himself translated the poets whom he loved. For him, faithfulness to the form was quite as important as faithfulness to the spirit, and Mr. Kamen has carried out his duty not merely with an understanding by which Pasternak would have been deeply touched, but with a dexterity which is all the more admirable because it is hidden by its own success.

C. M. BOWRA

CONTENTS

ix

II. WHEN THE SKIES CLEAR

III. LATER POEMS

TRANSLATOR'S NOTE

The poems in this volume represent all Pasternak's later work, and may therefore be reckoned the successor to *In early trains*, a small collection which the poet published in 1942. The present collection is divided into two sections, the first of which includes the poems of Doctor Zhivago, previously published as a part of the novel; and the second of which includes the full text of the cycle *When the Skies Clear* (*Kogda razgulyaetsya*). The circumstances in which the Zhivago text came to be published are now well known; the remainder of these poems emerged no less surreptitiously, circulating by hand, and brought out from Russia by private persons. A small number of them have been published in the Soviet Union: the literary journal *Znamya* published ten of the Zhivago poems in 1954, before the storm over the novel; and in 1956 *Znamya* also published eight of the *When the Skies Clear* collection. In both cases, certain significant revisions were made in the text. The entire canon of poems was to be called, according to Pasternak's own wishes, *In the Interlude* (*V Pereryve*): the title, with its stage-metaphor, and its personal hopes and fears, may be related to the mood of the opening Zhivago poem, *Hamlet*. It is difficult to date the earlier poems in this book, but certain of the Zhivago poems can probably be dated by their reference to events in Pasternak's own life. For the later poems in *When the Skies Clear* the poet supplied dates: the final four were written in January 1959, and the preceding six in the spring and summer of 1958. With these, Pasternak's poetic output apparently ends. There are few parallels for so prolonged a poetic life (his first volume was issued just before World War I), and the undimmed preservation and development of quality in Pasternak's poems.

These translations were completed two years ago, just before Pasternak's death. I have aimed primarily at exact translation, and have taken no liberties with meaning: the English is as close as possible. In the matter of form I have been more arbitrary, and followed the spirit of Pasternak's usage as well as my own inclination: a translator must be relatively free to compensate for what is inevitably lost by translation. The problem is an old one: in January 1959 Pasternak wrote to me that 'distressing features that I always try to forget in the original [poem], get revealed in translations in a desperately naked form'. The battle is lost before it is begun.

It remains to thank those who helped produce this book: Dr. George Katkov, who untiringly supervised my work, corrected my inadequate Russian, and fostered my enthusiasm; Mr. Max Hayward, for his constant help and advice; Sir Isaiah Berlin, for his unfailing encouragement; and Mrs. Marjorie Rear, who typed the text patiently and cheerfully.

H. K.

St. Antony's College
Oxford

I

THE POEMS OF YURY ZHIVAGO

СТИХОТВОРЕНИЯ ЮРИЯ ЖИВАГО

ГАМЛЕТ

Гул затих.   Я вышел на подмостки.
Прислонясь к дверному косяку,
Я ловлю в далеком отголоске
Что случится на моем веку.

На меня наставлен сумрак ночи
Тысячью биноклей на оси.
Если только можно, авва отче,
Чашу эту мимо пронеси.

Я люблю твой замысел упрямый
И играть согласен эту роль.
Но сейчас идет другая драма,
И на этот раз меня уволь.

Но продуман распорядок действий,
И неотвратим конец пути.
Я один, всё тонет в фарисействе.
Жизнь прожить — не поле перейти.

HAMLET

The tumult stills. I stand upon the stage
Against a door-post, dimly reckoning
From traces of a distantly-heard echo
What my unfinished lifetime may yet bring.

The black of night pours from these opera glasses
That in their thousands train their sights on me:
But Abba, Father, if it be your will,
Remove this chalice in your clemency.

Unswervingly your purpose holds my love,
This rôle you've set I am content to play;
But now a different drama takes the scene:
Spare me this once the treading of your way.

And yet the order of the acts is planned,
The way's end destinate and unconcealed.
Alone. Now is the time of Pharisees.
To live is not like walking through a field.

МАРТ

Солнце греет до седьмого пота,
И бушует, одурев овраг.
Как у дюжей скотницы работа,
Дело у весны кипит в руках.

Чахнет снег и болен малокровьем
В веточках бессильно синих жил.
Но дымится жизнь в хлеву коровьем,
И здоровьем пышут зубья вил.

Эти ночи, эти дни и ночи!
Дробь капелей к середине дня,
Кровельных сосулек худосочье,
Ручейков бессонных болтовня!

Настежь всё, конюшня и коровник.
Голуби в снегу клюют овес,
И всего живитель и виновник, —
Пахнет свежим воздухом навоз.

MARCH

The sun burns on perspiring earth,
The vale is live and blustering,
And work seethes in the able hands
Of that stout dairymaid, the spring.

Anaemic, wasting fast away,
The snow runs off in veins of blue,
But still the cowshed steams with life,
The pitchfork's teeth breathe health anew.

These nights, these passing days and nights!
At noon the thaw-beat on the pane,
The icicles' drip on the roof,
The constant stream's sleepless refrain!

The stables, cowshed, everything
Flung open wide! Birds pecking snow!
And freshness over all from dung
From which all life and causes flow!

НА СТРАСТНОЙ

Еще кругом ночная мгла.
Еще так рано в мире,
Что звездам в небе нет числа,
И каждая, как день, светла,
И если бы земля могла,
Она бы Пасху проспала
Под чтение псалтыри.

Еще кругом ночная мгла:
Такая рань на свете,
Что площадь вечностью легла
От перекрестка до угла,
И до рассвета и тепла
Еще тысячелетье.

Еще земля голым-гола,
И ей ночами не в чем
Раскачивать колокола
И вторить с воли певчим.

И со Страстного четверга
Вплоть до Страстной субботы
Вода буравит берега
И вьет водовороты.

И лес раздет и непокрыт,
И на Страстях Христовых,
Как строй молящихся, стоит
Толпой стволов сосновых.

IN HOLY WEEK

Around us still the dark of night
And still so early in the world
That stars unnumbered range the sky,
Each shining with the day's clear light,
And if it could the earth upcurled
Would wearily through Easter-tide
Sleep to the chanting of the Psalms.

Around us still the dark of night
And still so early in the world
That like eternity the square
Corner to crossroad is unfurled
And dawn and warmth are out of sight
More than a thousand years away.

And still the earth in nakedness
Has naught to wear by night to ring
The chapel bell out in response
To where inside the choirs sing.

And from Thursday of Holy Week
Till Holy Saturday begins
The water ploughs the river banks
And in its eddying whirlpools spins.

Stripped down and bare the forest rears,
And when Christ's Passion comes to pass
Its host of lofty pine-trees stand
Like worshippers attending Mass.

А в городе, на небольшом
Пространстве, как на сходке,
Деревья смотрят нагишом
В церковные решетки.

И взгляд их ужасом объят.
Понятна их тревога.
Сады выходят из оград,
Колеблется земли уклад:
Они хоронят Бога.

И видят свет у царских врат,
И черный плат, и свечек ряд,
Заплаканные лица —
И вдруг навстречу крестный ход
Выходит с плащаницей,
И две березы у ворот
Должны посторониться.

И шествие обходит двор
По краю тротуара,
И вносит с улицы в притвор
Весну, весенний разговор,
И воздух с привкусом просфор
И вешнего угара.

И март разбрасывает снег
На паперти толпе калек,
Как-будто вышел человек,
И вынес, и открыл ковчег,
И всё до нитки роздал.

And in the town where like a rally
They crowd together down the ways,
The trees in their pure nakedness
In through the church's gratings gaze.

And awe transfixes all their glances,
Alarm that you may well forgive,
For gardens burst out through their fences
And earth's foundations quake and move
And God is borne into the grave.

They see the light, the royal gate,
The rows of candles, the black pall,
The faces deeply stained with tears:
But suddenly before them all
A concourse with the shroud appears;
Two birches standing at the gate
Must bow aside to let them pass.

Round the yard goes the procession
And back along the pavement's edge,
To bear the spring, spring's conversation
Along the street into the porch,
And air with flavours of baked bread
And heady vapours of the spring.

Now March is scattering the snow
On groups of cripples in the porch
As though someone had brought the shrine
Outside, and to them, each and each,
Had given all he could bestow.

И пенье длится до зари,
И, нарыдавшись вдосталь,
Доходят тише изнутри
На пустыри под фонари
Псалтырь или апостол.

Но в полночь смолкнут тварь и плоть,
Заслышав слух весенний,
Что только-только распогодь,
Смерть можно будет побороть
Усильем воскресенья.

So lasts the singing till the dawn.
And when they cease their lengthy weep
The Psalms and Acts on silent feet
Now in the stillness softly creep
Into an empty, lamplit street.

And men and beasts at midnight hush
To hear this rumour in the spring,
That in the changing weather's hour
Death finds its only vanquishing
Through the Resurrection's power.

БЕЛАЯ НОЧЬ

Мне далекое время мерещится,
Дом на Стороне Петербургской.
Дочь степной небогатой помещицы,
Ты — на курсах, ты родом из Курска.

Ты — мила, у тебя есть поклонники.
Этой белою ночью мы оба,
Примостясь на твоем подоконнике,
Смотрим вниз с твоего небоскреба.

Фонари, точно бабочки газовые,
Утро тронуло первою дрожью.
То, что тихо тебе я рассказываю,
Так на спящие дали похоже.

Мы охвачены тою же самою
Оробелою верностью тайне,
Как раскинувшийся панорамою
Петербург за Невою бескрайней.

Там вдали, по дремучим урочищам,
Этой ночью весеннею белой,
Соловьи славословьем грохочущим
Оглашают лесные пределы.

Ошалелое щелканье катится,
Голос маленькой птички ледащей
Пробуждает восторг и сумятицу
В глубине очарованной чащи.

WHITE NIGHT

I dream again of that now distant past,
A house upon the Petersburgska Quai,
And you, a minor steppe landowner's daughter,
Were here from Kursk to spend your student days.

How charming in your ways, how young men loved you!
And once how we two through the long white night
Sat up together on your window-sill
And gazed below from that skyscraper height!

The street lamps, just like gaseous butterflies,
Would flicker when the morning touched their brows:
How softly came the words I spoke to you,
As softly as the distance's deep drowse!

And we, like Petersburg that sweeps away
Beyond the shoreless Neva's symmetry,
Were held within a secrecy of faith
To an immeasurable mystery.

And far beyond, out in the densest woods
Upon that white night of the radiant spring,
The nightingales were filling all the forest
Clear with the thunder of their praise-giving.

The madness of their trilling tumbled on:
The singing of the tiny, fragile bird
Aroused a strange and rapturous furore
Within the soul of the enchanted wood;

В те места босоногою странницей
Пробирается ночь вдоль забора,
И за ней с подоконника тянется
След подслушанного разговора.

В отголосках беседы услышанной
По садам, огороженным тесом,
Ветви яблоновые и вишенные
Одеваются цветом белесым.

И деревья, как призраки, белые
Высыпают толпой на дорогу,
Точно знаки прощальные делая
Белой ночи, видавшей так много.

While like a barefoot tramp the night crept there
In silence, close along the garden fences
And trailed behind it, from our window sill,
A wisp of overheard, soft sentences.

Where in the night their echo could be heard
Out in the garden not a trace of gloom
Remained where boughs of apple and of cherry
Burst suddenly into the whitest bloom;

And ghostly figures of the trees rose white
And poured into the road, across the scene,
As though to wave an ultimate farewell
Towards the white night and all it had seen.

ВЕСЕННЯЯ РАСПУТИЦА

Огни заката догорали.
Распутицей в бору глухом
В далекийхутор на Урале
Тащился человек верхом.

Болтала лошадь селезенкой
И звону шлепавших подков
Дорогой вторила вдогонку
Вода в воронках родников.

Когда же опускал поводья
И шагом ехал верховой,
Прокатывало половодье
Вблизи весь гул и грохот свой.

Смеялся кто-то, плакал кто-то,
Крошились камни о кремни,
И падали в водовороты
С корнями вырванные пни.

А на пожарище заката,
В далекой прочерни ветвей,
Как гулкий колокол набата
Неистовствовал соловей.

Где ива вдовий свой повойник
Клонила, свесивши в овраг,
Как древний соловей-разбойник
Свистал он на семи дубах.

SPRING FLOODS

The fires of the sunset died away
As in the slush and through the wood
Towards a solitary Urals farm
A weary horseman slowly rode.

His horse champed in impatient rage,
And as the ringing horseshoes galloped by,
Within the hollow-echoed streams
The water followed with its clear reply.

The rider loosed his reins and slowed the horse
Down to a walk along the road;
In thunder echoing throughout the fields
The furious spring flood rolled and flowed.

Somewhere someone now laughed, now wept:
Stone sharply ground on stone upon his ride
As stumps uprooted from the earth
Crashed down into the swiftly eddying tide;

While in the splendid dying of the sun,
The distant coal-black foliage,
Like some reverberating tocsin's call
A nightingale distilled its rage:

And where the weeping-willow dipped
Its widows weeds above the hollow nooks,
Just like the Robber-Nightingale
It whistled as it sat on seven oaks.

Какой беде, какой зазнобе
Предназначался этот пыл?
В кого ружейной крупной дробью
Он по чащобе запустил?

Казалось, вот он выйдет лешим
С привала беглых каторжан
Навстречу конным или пешим
Заставам здешних партизан.

Земля и небо, лес и поле
Ловили этот редкий звук,
Размеренные эти доли
Безумья, боли, счастья, мук.

For what misfortune then, or for what love
Was poured out all this violence?
At whom among the thickets of the wood
Was aimed this grapeshot's incidence?

And now, it seemed, the bird would come
Like an hobgoblin from its convict's lair
To meet the horse and foot patrols
Of local partisans assembled there.

All earth, the sky, the forest and the field,
Enmeshed the torment and the pain,
The madness and the happiness that shared
And blended in that rare refrain.

ОБЪЯСНЕНИЕ

Жизнь вернулась так же беспричинно
Как когда-то странно прервалась.
Я на той же улице старинной,
Как тогда, в тот летний день и час.

Те же люди и заботы те же,
И пожар заката не остыл,
Как его тогда к стене Манежа
Вечер смерти наспех пригвоздил.

Женщины в дешевом затрапезе
Так же ночью топчут башмаки.
Их потом на кровельном железе
Так же распинают чердаки.

Вот одна походкою усталой
Медленно выходит на порог
И, поднявшись из полуподвала,
Переходит двор наискосок.

Я опять готовлю отговорки,
И опять всё безразлично мне.
И соседка, обогнув задворки,
Оставляет нас наедине.

* * *

Не плачь, не морщь опухших губ,
Не собирай их в складки.
Разбередишь присохший струп
Весенней лихорадки.

EXPLANATION

Life has returned as inexplicably
As when it once so strangely broke away
And I am in the same old antique street
As then, upon that summer hour and day.

The selfsame people here, the selfsame cares;
Nor has the sunset's flame begun to fall
Since that once when the low twilight of death
Nailed it in haste upon the Manège wall.

These women in their shabby cotton dresses
Still wear their shoes out through the long night-tide
And then upon the iron of the roof
Lie in their attics to be crucified.

How wearily now this one takes her steps
Slowly towards the threshold and the door
And struggles upward from the basement depths
To cut obliquely through the yard once more!

And I prepare again my neat excuses
And lapse into an apathetic tone;
And once again the woman from next door
Goes round the alley, leaving us alone.

*　　*　　*

Don't cry, don't purse your swollen lips,
Don't keep them puckering,
You'll crack the dryness of the scabs
Caused by the acne in the spring!

Сними ладонь с моей груди,
Мы провода под током.
Друг к другу вновь, того гляди,
Нас бросит ненароком,

Пройдут года, ты вступишь в брак,
Забудешь неустройства.
Быть женщиной — великий шаг,
Сводить с ума — геройство.

А я пред чудом женских рук,
Спины, и плеч, и шеи,
И так с привязанностью слуг
Весь век благоговею.

Но как ни сковывает ночь
Меня кольцом тоскливым,
Сильней на свете тяга прочь
И манит страсть к разрывам.

And take your hand off from my breast:
For we are both high-tension wires;
Look out, or we may yet again
Be thrown together unawares!

The years will pass, you'll marry and
Forget these wayward days you had:
How great it is to be a woman!
Heroic—to drive others mad!

For me, these wondrous woman's hands,
Back, shoulders, neck, hold my intense
And still subservient devotion:
I pay my lifelong reverence.

And though the night may forge and weld
Its chains of grief to make me stay,
The world's opposing pull is stronger,
And passion carries me away!

ЛЕТО В ГОРОДЕ

Разговоры вполголоса
И с поспешностью пылкой
Кверху собраны волосы
Всей копною с затылка.

Из-под гребня тяжелого
Смотрит женщина в шлеме,
Запрокинувши голову
Вместе с косами всеми.

А на улице жаркая
Ночь сулит непогоду,
И расходятся, шаркая,
По домам пешеходы.

Гром отрывистый слышится,
Отдающийся резко,
И от ветра колышится
На окне занавеска.

Наступает безмолвие,
Но попрежнему парит.
И попрежнему молнии
В небе шарят и шарят.

А когда светозарное
Утро знойное снова
Сушит лужи бульварные
После ливня ночного,

Смотрят хмуро по случаю
Своего недосыпа
Вековые, пахучие,
Неотцветшие липы.

SUMMER IN TOWN

The voices lowered as we talk:
And the entire sheaf of hair
Raised in a flourish from the neck
But with a hasty lack of care:

Yet, underneath the heavy comb
A woman in a helmet looks—
The backward tossing of her head
As all its plaited wonder shakes!

And outside in the street the heat,
The hot night, presages a storm;
As, scattering, shuffling along,
The passers-by make their way home.

A crack of thunder cuts across
And echoes sharply, while the blind
That's draped before the window pane
Is stirred and fidgets with the wind.

Now again the silence moves up
But hovers over sultrily,
Now again the lightning's fingers
Still search and search across the sky;

And when, pierced through with early dawn,
The heavy morning once again
Has dried the puddled avenues
After a night of steady rain,

The centuried, the sweet-perfumed
Lime trees hung high with blossoms keep
A frown upon their lissom boughs,
Complaining of their lack of sleep.

ВЕТЕР

Я кончился, а ты жива.
И ветер, жалуясь и плача,
Раскачивает лес и дачу.
Не каждую сосну отдельно,
А полностью все дерева
Со всею далью беспредельной
Как парусников кузова
На глади бухты корабельной.
И это не из удальства
Или из ярости бесцельной,
А чтоб в тоске найти слова
Тебе для песни колыбельной.

THE WIND

My end has come but you live on.
The wind weeps out its plaintive cry
And rocks the house and forest round
And pine-trees, yet not one by one,
But all together waving high
Into and with the vast beyond
Like hulls of sailing ships that lie
And ride at anchor in a bay;
And this not for a whim or two,
Nor yet in blind malignity,
But from its grief to spin for you
The soft words of a lullaby.

ХМЕЛЬ

Под ракитой, обвитой плющом,
От ненастья мы ищем защиты.
Наши плечи покрыты плащем,
Вкруг тебя мои руки обвиты.

Я ошибся. Кусты этих чащ
Не плющом перевиты, а хмелем.
Ну так лучше давай этот плащ
В ширину под собою расстелем.

INTOXICATION

Here's ivy round this willow tree
That hides us from the driving rain:
A cape encloses you and me,
My arms enclose you in their chain.

And yet . . . it is not ivy here
But hops that twine the bushes round:
Oh, how much finer if we spread
This cape to bed us on the ground!

БАБЬЕ ЛЕТО

Лист смородины груб и матерчат.
В доме хохот и стекла звенят,
В нем шинкуют, и квасят, и перчат,
И гвоздики кладут в маринад.

Лес забрасывает, как насмешник,
Этот шум на обрывистый склон,
Где сгоревший на солнце орешник,
Словно жаром костра опален.

Здесь дорога спускается в балку,
Здесь и высохших старых коряг,
И лоскутницы осени жалко,
Всё сметающей в этот овраг.

И того, что вселенная проще,
Чем иной полагает хитрец,
Что как в воду опущена роща,
Что приходит всему свой конец.

Что глазами бессмысленно хлопать,
Когда всё пред тобой сожжено,
И осенняя белая копоть
Паутиною тянет в окно.

Ход из сада в заборе проломан
И теряется в березняке.
В доме смех и хозяйственный гомон,
Тот же гомон и смех вдалеке.

INDIAN SUMMER

The blackcurrant leaf is canvas and coarse,
There's laughter at home, the ringing of glass,
Everyone slicing, pickling and peppering
And busily bottling cloves into jars.

The forest in mockery scatters afar
Along the steep slope its echoes of sound
To where the hazel bush, scorched in the sun,
Like some old camp fire burns on the ground.

And here is a path that leads down the gully:
Our sorrow swells here for dry, fallen trees,
And autumn—a ragged, desolate man
Who sweeps down everything into the leas;

And sorrow the world is somehow far simpler
Than many all-knowing people pretend;
With sorrow for boughs with hang-dogged looks
And sorrow that all things come to an end;

That there is no point in just gazing blankly
When all that's before you burns into air,
And white soot comes falling out of the autumn
Then drifts through the window like cobwebs, like hair.

A path in the garden cuts through the fence
And into the birchwood loses its way;
As laughter and din ring out through the house
The same din and laughter ring far away.

СВАДЬБА

Пересекши край двора,
Гости на гулянку
В дом невесты до утра
Перешли с тальянкой.

За хозяйскими дверьми
В войлочной обивке
Стихли с часу до семи
Болтовни обрывки.

А зарею, в самый сон,
Только спать и спать бы,
Вновь запел акордеон,
Уходя со свадьбы.

И рассыпал гармонист
Снова на баяне
Плеск ладоней, блеск монист,
Шум и гам гулянья.

И опять, опять, опять
Говорок частушки
Прямо к спящим на кровать
Ворвался с пирушки.

А одна, как снег, бела,
В шуме, свисте, гаме
Снова павой поплыла,
Поводя боками,

Помавая головой
И рукою правой,
В плясовой по мостовой,
Павой, павой, павой.

THE WEDDING PARTY

Across the yard the guests
Come visiting the bride
To feast within her house
Until the morningtide:

Behind the landlord's firm
And heavy baize-lined door
From one o'clock till seven
There's chattering no more.

But when at dawn you wish
Just to keep sleeping still,
Then the accordion
Leaves, with a merry will:

Again the player hurls
His music to the throng,
Palms clapping, sparkling beads,
The hubbub and the song!

Again, again, again
The dancing rhythms creep
Straight from the party crowd
To where the others sleep.

And white as snow a girl
Fair as a peacock flows
Through whistles and applause,
Hips swaying as she goes,—

And waving of her hand,
Head nodding, and her glancing,
Peacock on the pavement,—
Dancing, dancing, dancing!

Вдруг задор и шум игры,
Топот хоровода,
Провалясь в тартарары,
Канули, как в воду.

Просыпался шумный двор.
Деловое эхо
Вмешивалось в разговор
И раскаты смеха.

В необъятность неба, ввысь
Вихрем сизых пятен
Стаей голуби неслись,
Снявшись с голубятен.

Точно их за свадьбой вслед,
Спохватясь спросонья,
С пожеланьем многих лет
Выслали в погоню.

Жизнь ведь тоже только миг,
Только растворенье
Нас самих во всех других
Как бы им в даренье.

Только свадьба, вглубь окон
Рвущаяся снизу,
Только песня, только сон,
Только голубь сизый.

But suddenly the swing
Of song, the furious
Dance, sink down as through water,
Drop through to Tartarus.

The noisy yard awakes;
And echoes follow after
Of business mixed with talk
And with the peals of laughter.

While, grey-blue in a whirlwind
A flock of pigeons fly
In fury from their dovecotes
Up to an endless sky,

As though someone just waking
Had sent belated cheers
To wish the wedding party
A life of happy years.

For life is but a moment,
Is only a dissolving
Of ourselves into others,
Life is simply a giving,

A wedding feast that bursts
Through windows from the light,
Merely a song, a dream,
A grey-blue pigeon's flight.

ОСЕНЬ

Я дал разъехаться домашним,
Все близкие давно в разброде,
И одиночеством всегдашним
Полно всё в сердце и природе.

И вот я здесь с тобой в сторожке,
В лесу безлюдно и пустынно.
Как в песне, стежки и дорожки
Позаросли наполовину.

Теперь на нас одних с печалью
Глядят бревенчатые стены.
Мы брать преград не обещали,
Мы будем гибнуть откровенно.

Мы сядем в час и встанем в третьем,
Я с книгою, ты с вышиваньем,
И на рассвете не заметим,
Как целоваться перестанем.

Еще пышней и бесшабашней
Шумите, осыпайтесь, листья,
И чашу горечи вчерашней
Сегодняшней тоской превысьте.

Привязанность, влеченье, прелесть!
Рассеемся в сентябрьском шуме!
Заройся вся в осенний шелест!
Замри, или ополоумей!

AUTUMN

I have allowed my family to scatter,
All those who were my dearest to depart,
And once again an age-long loneliness
Comes in to fill all nature and my heart.

Alone this cottage shelters me and you:
The wood is an unpeopled wilderness
And ways and footpaths wear, as in the song,
Weeds almost overgrowing each recess;

And where we sit together by ourselves
The log walls gaze upon us mournfully.
We gave no promise to leap obstacles,
We shall yet face our end with honesty.

At one we'll sit, at three again we'll rise,
My book with me, your sewing in your hand,
Nor with the dawning shall we realize
When all our kissing shall have had an end.

You leaves, more richly and more recklessly
Rustle your dresses, spill yourselves away,
And fill a past day's cup of bitterness
Still higher with the anguish of today!

All this delight, devotion and desire!
We'll fling ourselves into September's riot!
Immure yourself within the autumn's rustle
Entirely: go crazy, or be quiet!

Ты так же сбрасываешь платье,
Как роща сбрасывает листья,
Когда ты падаешь в объятье
В халате с шелковою кистью.

Ты — благо гибельного шага,
Когда житье тошней недуга,
А корень красоты — отвага,
И это тянет нас друг к другу.

How when you fall into my gentle arms
Enrobed in that silk-tasselled dressing gown
You shake the dress you wear away from you
As only coppices shake their leaves down!—

You are the blessing on my baneful way,
When life has depths worse than disease can reach,
And courage is the only root of beauty,
And it is this that draws us each to each.

СКАЗКА

Встарь, во время оно,
В сказочном краю
Пробирался конный
Степью по репью.

Он спешил на сечу,
А в степной пыли
Темный лес навстречу
Вырастал вдали.

Ныло ретивое,
На сердце скребло:
Бойся водопоя,
Подтяни седло.

Не послушал конный
И во весь опор
Залетел с разгону
На лесной бугор.

Повернул с кургана,
Въехал в суходол,
Миновал поляну,
Гору перешел.

И забрел в ложбину
И лесной тропой
Вышел на звериный
След и водопой.

И глухой к призыву,
И не вняв чутью,
Свел коня с обрыва
Попоить к ручью.

*　*　*

A FAIRY TALE

Once in olden ages
In a faery land
Rode a horseman, spurring
Through the rough steppe-land.

As he sped to battle
Through the dust a dim
Distant and dark forest
Rose ahead of him.

An uneasy feeling
Troubled him a space:
'Tighten up your saddle,
Fear the watering-place.'

But he would not listen,
Only sped at will
Swiftly at a gallop
Up the wooded hill;

Turning from the hillock
Through a dried-up rill,
Rode around a meadow
And across a hill;

Came into a hollow,
Found a path to ride
Following a beast's spoor
To the waterside;

Deaf then to all warning
And without remorse,
To the waterside he
Down-dale led his horse.

*   *   *

У ручья пещера,
Пред пещерой — брод.
Как бы пламя серы
Озаряло вход.

И в дыму багровом,
Застилавшем взор,
Отдаленным зовом
Огласился бор.

И тогда оврагом,
Вздрогнув, напрямик
Тронул конный шагом
На призывный крик.

И увидел конный,
И приник к копью,
Голову дракона,
Хвост и чешую.

Пламенем из зева
Рассевал он свет,
В три кольца вкруг девы
Обмотав хребет.

Туловище змея,
Как концом бича,
Поводило шеей
У ее плеча.

Той страны обычай
Пленницу-красу
Отдавал в добычу
Чудищу в лесу.

But across the shallow
Stream a cavern lay,
To whose entrance sulphur
Flames lit up the way,

While the blood-red smoke fumes
Clouded up his eyes . . .
Sudden through the pinewood
Sounded distant cries!

Then the rider started
In that valley's thrall
And he moved ahead in
Answer to the call,

Till he saw before him,
As he couched his spear,
Gaunt head of a dragon,
Tail and scales of fear.

Light was scattered round as
In its jaws flame boiled:
Thrice around a maiden
Was its body coiled.

Like a whip's tail curling,
Now the monstrous snake
Round the maiden's shoulders
Swayed its scaly neck.

By that country's custom
Was a ransom made
To the monster, of a
Lovely captive maid:

Края населенье
Хижины свои
Выкупало пеней
Этой от змеи.

Змей обвил ей руку
И оплел гортань,
Получив на муку
В жертву эту дань.

Посмотрел с мольбою
Всадник в высь небес
И копье для боя
Взял на перевес.

*   *   *

Сомкнутые веки.
Выси.   Облака.
Воды.   Броды.   Реки.
Годы и века.

Конный в шлеме сбитом,
Сшибленный в бою.
Верный конь, копытом
Топчущий змею.

Конь и труп дракона
Рядом на песке.
В обмороке конный,
Дева в столбняке.

So great was the tribute
That the people paid
For the beast to leave their
Hovels undismayed.

Turning on the victim
Given to her fate,
In its coils the dragon
Wrapped her arms and throat.

With a prayer the rider
Glanced up to the sky
Then prepared for battle,
Levelled his spear high.

*   *   *

Eyelids tightly closing,
Heights and clouds in tiers,
Waters, fords, and rivers,
Centuries and years!

Hurled down with his helmet
He is hurt and thrown,
But his faithful charger
Treads the serpent down.

Steed, and dragon's body,
In the dust are laid;
Senseless lies the rider,
In a trance the maid.

Светел свод полдневный,
Синева нежна.
Кто она? Царевна?
Дочь земли? Княжна?

То, в избытке счастья
Слезы в три ручья,
То душа во власти
Сна и забытья.

То возврат здоровья,
То недвижность жил
От потери крови
И упадка сил.

Но сердца их бьются.
То она, то он
Силятся очнуться
И впадают в сон.

Сомкнутые веки.
Выси. Облака.
Воды. Броды. Реки.
Годы и века.

Noonday's heaven flashes
Sky-blue tenderness:
Who is she?   A lady?
Peasant girl?   Princess?

Now joy overwhelms them
So much that they weep,
Now their souls succumb to
An oblivious sleep.

Now comes strength returning,
And now motionless
Lies the rider, weakened
By his life-blood's loss.

But their hearts are beating
And now he, now she,
Struggling to awaken
Falls back sleepily.

Eyelids tightly closing,
Heights and clouds in tiers,
Waters, fords, and rivers,
Centuries and years!

АВГУСТ

Как обещало, не обманывая,
Проникло солнце утром рано
Косою полосой шафрановою
От занавеси до дивана.

Оно покрыло жаркой охрою
Соседний лес, дома поселка,
Мою постель, подушку мокрую
И край стены за книжной полкой.

Я вспомнил, по какому поводу
Слегка увлажнена подушка.
Мне снилось, что ко мне на проводы
Шли по лесу вы друг за дружкой.

Вы шли толпою, врозь и парами,
Вдруг кто-то вспомнил, что сегодня
Шестое августа по старому,
Преображение Господне.

Обыкновенно свет без пламени
Исходит в этот день с Фавора,
И осень, ясная как знаменье,
К себе приковывает взоры.

И вы прошли сквозь мелкий, нищенский,
Нагой, трепещущий ольшаник
В имбирно-красный лес кладбищенский,
Горевший, как печатный пряник.

AUGUST

This was its promise, held to faithfully:
The early morning sun came in this way
Until the angle of its saffron beam
Between the curtains and the sofa lay,

And with its ochre heat it spread across
The village houses, and the nearby wood,
Upon my bed and on my dampened pillow
And to the corner where the bookcase stood.

Then I recalled the reason why my pillow
Had been so dampened by those tears that fell—
I'd dreamt I saw you coming one by one
Across the wood to wish me your farewell.

You came in ones and twos, a straggling crowd;
Then suddenly someone mentioned a word:
It was the sixth of August, by Old Style,
And the Transfiguration of Our Lord.

For from Mount Tabor usually this day
There comes a light without a flame to shine,
And autumn draws all eyes upon itself
As clear and unmistaken as a sign.

But you came forward through the tiny, stripped,
The pauperly and trembling alder grove,
Into the graveyard's coppice, russet-red,
Which, like stamped gingerbread, lay there and glowed.

С притихшими его вершинами
Соседствовало небо важно,
И голосами петушиными
Перекликалась даль протяжно.

В лесу казенной землемершею
Стояла смерть среди погоста,
Смотря в лицо мое умершее,
Чтоб вырыть яму мне по росту.

Был всеми ощутим физически
Спокойный голос чей-то рядом.
То прежний голос мой провидческий
Звучал, нетронутый распадом:

«Прощай, лазурь преображенская
И золото второго Спаса.
Смягчи последней лаской женскою
Мне горечь рокового часа.

Прощайте, годы безвременщины.
Простимся, бездне унижений
Бросающая вызов женщина!
Я — поле твоего сраженья.

Прощай, размах крыла расправленный,
Полета вольное упорство,
И образ мира, в слове явленный,
И творчество, и чудотворство».

And with the silence of those high treetops
Was neighbour only the imposing sky
And in the echoed crowing of the cocks
The distances and distances rang by:

There in the churchyard underneath the trees,
Like some surveyor from the government
Death gazed on my pale face to estimate
How large a grave would suit my measurement.

All those who stood there could distinctly hear
A quiet voice emerge from where I lay:
The voice was mine, my past; prophetic words
That sounded now, unsullied by decay:

'Farewell, wonder of azure and of gold
Surrounding the Transfiguration's power:
Assuage now with a woman's last caress
The bitterness of my predestined hour!

'Farewell timeless expanse of passing years!
Farewell, woman who flung your challenge steeled
Against the abyss of humiliations:
For it is I who am your battlefield!

'Farewell, you span of open wings outspread,
The voluntary obstinacy of flight,
O figure of the world revealed in speech,
Creative genius, wonder-working might!'

ЗИМНЯЯ НОЧЬ

Мело, мело по всей земле
Во все пределы.
Свеча горела на столе,
Свеча горела.

Как летом роем мошкара
Летит на пламя,
Слетались хлопья со двора
К оконной раме.

Метель лепила на стекле
Кружки и стрелы.
Свеча горела на столе,
Свеча горела.

На озаренный потолок
Ложились тени,
Скрещенья рук, скрещенья ног,
Судьбы скрещенья.

И падали два башмачка
Со стуком на пол.
И воск слезами с ночника
На платье капал.

И всё терялось в снежной мгле
Седой и белой.
Свеча горела на столе,
Свеча горела.

WINTER NIGHT

Sweeping, sweeping all earth's corners
Came the snowstorm turning;
On the table burned a candle,
Stood a candle burning.

As in summer swarms of midges
Draw towards the flame,
From outside there flocked the snowflakes
To the window pane.

On the window circles, arrows,
Marked the snowstorm's churning;
On the table burned a candle,
Stood a candle burning.

And across the brightened ceiling
Fell the shadows' spate:
Arms cross-wise and legs cross-wise
In a cross-wise fate.

With a thud upon the floor
A pair of shoes fell down;
Waxen teardrops from the night-light
Dripped upon a gown.

All was lost in snowy darkness,
In the white hoar whirling.
On the table burned a candle,
Stood a candle burning.

На свечку дуло из угла,
И жар соблазна
Вздымал, как ангел, два крыла
Крестообразно.

Мело весь месяц в феврале,
И то и дело
Свеча горела на столе,
Свеча горела.

Corner-draughts caught at the flame
As temptation's fire
Raised a pair of angels' wings
Like a cross afire.

All through February the snow swept:
Sometimes in its turning
On the table burned a candle,
Stood a candle burning.

РАЗЛУКА

С порога смотрит человек,
Не узнавая дома.
Ее отъезд был как побег.
Везде следы разгрома.

Повсюду в комнате хаос.
Он меры разоренья
Не замечает из-за слез
И приступа мигрени.

В ушах с утра какой-то шум.
Он в памяти иль грезит?
И почему ему на ум
Всё мысль о море лезет?

Когда сквозь иней на окне
Не видно света божья,
Безвыходность тоски вдвойне
С пустыней моря схожа.

Она была так дорога
Ему чертой любою,
Как морю близки берега
Всей линией прибоя.

Как затопляет камыши
Волненье после шторма,
Ушли на дно его души
Ее черты и формы.

PARTING

He comes into the door and sees
A house he cannot recognize
For her departure looks like flight
And all around its havoc lies:

The rooms are in an utter chaos;
Yet still he cannot realize
The measure of his abject loss,
For throbbing head and tear-filled eyes.

Since dawn a roar has filled his ears.
Is he awake?—his dreams run free.
And why does his mind surge with thoughts
Incessant of the sounding sea?

When earth's unlimited expanse
Is frost-obscured upon the pane,
Then more are deserts of the sea
Like sorrow's hopelessness, its pain:

How all her features were to him
As close, as dear undyingly,
As every breaker on the shore
Is close to the undying sea!

As, after storms, the surge flows up
And covers reeds within its deep,
So all her features drown in him:
Their hidden image he will keep.

В года мытарств, во времена
Немыслимого быта
Она волной судьбы со дна
Была к нему прибита.

Среди препятствий без числа,
Опасности минуя,
Волна несла ее, несла
И пригнала вплотную.

И вот теперь ее отъезд,
Насильственный, быть может,
Разлука их обоих съест,
Тоска с костями сгложет.

И человек глядит кругом:
Она в момент ухода
Всё выворотила вверх дном
Из ящиков комода.

Он бродит, и до темноты
Укладывает в ящик
Раскиданные лоскуты
И выкройки образчик.

И наколовшись об шитье
С невынутой иголкой,
Внезапно видит всю ее
И плачет втихомолку.

In years of trial when life's flow
Most was unbearable and dim,
The sea-depths and the tide of fate
Then washed her up, brought her to him.

Despite the countless obstacles
Within the ocean's threatening roar
Still narrowly the homing tide
Held her and bore her safe ashore:

And now she's left and gone away,
Perhaps even against her will;
This parting will devour, the pain
Will gnaw into their bones, and kill.

He looks around him at the house
In which, only a while before
She left, she ransacked everything,
Turned out each cupboard and each drawer.

Till darkness falls he moods about
And places in drawers carefully
Scraps scattered idly on the floor,
Patterns she used for tracery;

And pricks himself upon a needle
Where some of her embroidery lies—
Then suddenly he sees her all
And quiet tears come to his eyes.

СВИДАНИЕ

Засыпет снег дороги,
Завалит скаты крыш.
Пойду размять я ноги:
За дверью ты стоишь.

Одна в пальто осеннем,
Без шляпы, без калош,
Ты борешься с волненьем
И мокрый снег жуешь.

Деревья и ограды
Уходят вдаль, во мглу.
Одна средь снегопада
Стоишь ты на углу.

Течет вода с косынки
За рукава в обшлаг,
И каплями росинки
Сверкают в волосах.

И прядью белокурой
Озарены: лицо,
Косынка и фигура
И это пальтецо.

Снег на ресницах влажен,
В твоих глазах тоска,
И весь твой облик слажен
Из одного куска.

MEETING

When snow lies covering the roads,
And makes the roofs its floor,
I'll start out for a walk—and see
You standing at the door;

Alone, in your autumnal coat,
Bare-haired, bootless, you stand:
You struggle with your thoughts, and chew
The damp snow in your hand.

Far out into the distant dark
Trees, fences fade away:
Alone amid the falling snow
Disconsolate you stay.

The water from your scarf rolls down
Your sleeves and lingers there:
Like morning dew the little drops
Now sparkle in your hair;

And suddenly a shining wisp
Of hair lights up your face:
It tints your scarf, your shabby coat,
Your figure's fragile grace.

The snow is wet upon your lashes,
There's anguish in your eyes,
But every feature of your face
Is a unique surprise.

Как-будто бы железом
Обмокнутым в сурьму
Тебя вели нарезом
По сердцу моему.

И в нем навек засело
Смиренье этих черт.
И оттого нет дела,
Что свет жестокосерд.

И оттого двоится
Вся эта ночь в снегу,
И провести границы
Меж нас я не могу.

Но кто мы и откуда,
Когда от всех тех лет
Остались пересуды,
А нас на свете нет?

As with an iron chisel
Dipped in antimony,
So clearly on my heart are you
Engraved undyingly,

And in it will for ever live
Your eyes' humility;
Be then the hard world merciless—
It has no claims on me.

And therefore this wide night of snow
Resolves itself in two:
I cannot draw the frontiers
Dividing me from you.

But who are we, and whence are we,
When of those long years' space
Only the idle words are left,
And of us not a trace?

РОЖДЕСТВЕНСКАЯ ЗВЕЗДА

Стояла зима.
Дул ветер из степи.
И холодно было младенцу в вертепе
На склоне холма.

Его согревало дыханье вола.
Домашние звери
Стояли в пещере,
Над яслями теплая дымка плыла.

Доху отряхнув от постельной трухи
И зернышек проса,
Смотрели с утеса
Спросонья в полночную даль пастухи.

Вдали было поле в снегу и погост,
Ограды, надгробья,
Оглобля в сугробе,
И небо над кладбищем, полное звезд.

А рядом, неведомая перед тем,
Застенчивей плошки
В оконце сторожки
Мерцала звезда по пути в Вифлеем.

Она пламенела, как стог, в стороне
От неба и бога,
Как отблеск поджога,
Как хутор в огне и пожар на гумне.

Она возвышалась горящей скирдой
Соломы и сена
Средь целой вселенной,
Встревоженной этою новой звездой.

CHRISTMAS STAR

A wind was blowing from the steppe
In that deep wintertide
Where in a cold cave slept a child
Upon the curved hillside.

An ox's breath was all his warmth
And every farmyard beast
Beneath the warm haze of the cave
Was stabled and at rest;

While, shaking hay-seed from their coats
Which they drew round them tight,
Some drowsy shepherds from their rock
Gazed far into the night

At fences, and a field in snow,
A cart snowed up for hours,
A cemetery, and over it
A heavenful of stars.

And, shyer than a watchman's light,
Nor till now seen by them,
A star rose shining on its way
That led to Bethlehem.

It flamed out like a haystack, far
Away from God and sky,
As though it were a farm ablaze,
A fire sparkling high

Which rose up like a flaming rick
Of burning thatch and hay
Amid a startled universe
That saw the new star's way.

Растущее зарево рдело над ней
И значило что-то,
И три звездочета
Спешили на зов небывалых огней.

За ними везли на верблюдах дары.
И ослики в сбруе, один малорослей
Другого, шажками спускались с горы.

И странным виденьем грядущей поры
Вставало вдали всё пришедшее после.
Все мысли веков, все мечты, все миры,
Всё будущее галлерей и музеев,
Все шалости фей, все дела чародеев,
Все елки на свете, все сны детворы.

Весь трепет затепленных свечек, все цепи,
Всё великолепье цветной мишуры . . .
. . . Всё злей и свирепей дул ветер из степи . . .
. . . Все яблоки, все золотые шары.

Часть пруда скрывали верхушки ольхи,
Но часть было видно отлично отсюда
Сквозь гнезда грачей и деревьев верхи.
Как шли вдоль запруды ослы и верблюды,
Могли хорошо разглядеть пастухи.
— Пойдемте со всеми, поклонимся чуду, —
Сказали они, запахнув кожухи.

От шарканья по снегу сделалось жарко.
По яркой поляне листами слюды
Вели за хибарку босые следы.
На эти следы, как на пламя огарка,
Ворчали овчарки при свете звезды.

Its red glow deepened as it rose—
A signal in the night—
And three star-gazers sped to its
Unprecedented light.

Behind them, camels bearing gifts,
And just two donkeys, followed till
Their mincing steps came down the hill.

But, in strange visions of the flow of time,
All future ages rose up distantly,
The thoughts, hopes, worlds, of every century,
The life of museums, art galleries,
All magic deeds, and every fairy whim,
Each childhood dream, and all the bright fir trees;

The candles glimmering, the paper chains,
The coloured tinsel sparkling in array,
. . . A wind blew fierce and wilder from the plains . . .
The apples, bubbles in a golden spray.

The alder-heads obscured part of the pool
Though some of it could be distinctly seen
Between the rooks' nests and the tops of trees.
The watching shepherds could make out with ease
Donkeys and camels moving past the well;
They wrapped their sheepskins tight, deciding then,
'Let's go with them to greet the miracle.'

And warmth rose as they shuffled through the snow
Where, on the bright plain, glittering like glass,
Their bare footprints led round behind a hut,
And at these, as at burning candle ends,
The sheepdogs growled about beneath the stars.

Морозная ночь походила на сказку,
И кто-то с навьюженной снежной гряды
Всё время незримо входил в их ряды.
Собаки брели, озираясь с опаской,
И жались к подпаску, и ждали беды.

По той же дороге, чрез эту же местность
Шло несколько ангелов в гуще толпы.
Незримыми делала их бестелесность,
Но шаг оставлял отпечаток стопы.

У камня толпилась орава народу.
Светало.   Означились кедров стволы.
— А кто вы такие? — спросила Мария.
— Мы племя пастушье и неба послы,
Пришли вознести вам обоим хвалы.
— Всем вместе нельзя.   Подождите у входа.

Средь серой, как пепел, предутренней мглы
Топтались погонщики и овцеводы,
Ругались со всадниками пешеходы,
У выдолбленной водопойной колоды
Ревели верблюды, лягались ослы.

Светало.   Рассвет, как пылинки золы,
Последние звезды сметал с небосвода.
И только волхвов из несметного сброда
Впустила Мария в отверстье скалы.

Он спал, весь сияющий, в яслях из дуба
Как месяца луч в углубленье дупла.
Ему заменяли овчинную шубу
Ослиные губы и ноздри вола.

The frosty dark was like a fairy tale
As from the driving snowdrifts through the night
Some unseen beings joined them on the trail,
And dogs that followed looked round warily
Behind their boy, for trouble or a fight.

By this same road, and through this countryside,
Went several angels hidden in the crowd,
So unsubstantial they could not be spied,
Invisible, and just their footprints shewed.

A crowd of people clustered round the cave
As day dawned and the cedar trunks rose clear;
'Who are you?'   Mary asked when they arrived.
'A shepherd tribe and heaven's ambassadors
Who bring our praise to offer to you here.'
'You cannot all come in, so wait outside.'

And in the ash-grey dark before the dawn
Herdsmen and shepherds stamped about outside
While those on horse and foot swore at each other
And by the hollow wooden water trough
The camels snorted loud, the asses shied.

When day broke, and like dusty flecks of ash
Dawn swept the last stars from a greying sky,
Out of the multitude assembled there
Mary let in only the three Magi.

He slept there radiant in his oaken cot
Like moonlight in the hollow of a tree:
Instead of sheepskin, only asses' lips
And breath of oxen warmed him tenderly.

Стояли в тени, словно в сумраке хлева,
Шептались, едва подбирая слова.
Вдруг кто-то в потемках, немного налево
От яслей рукой отодвинул волхва,
И тот оглянулся: с порога на деву
Как гостья, смотрела звезда Рождества.

They stood in shadow in that cattle-stall
And whispered, lost in awe at what to say,
When suddenly a hand came from the dark
And moved one of them gently from the way:
He looked around; there, like a guest, afar
Upon the Virgin gazed the Christmas Star.

РАССВЕТ

Ты значил всё в моей судьбе.
Потом пришла война, разруха
И долго-долго о тебе
Ни слуху не было, ни духу.

И через много-много лет
Твой голос вновь меня встревожил.
Всю ночь читал я твой завет
И как от обморока ожил.

Мне к людям хочется, в толпу,
В их утреннее оживленье.
Я всё готов разнесть в щепу
И всех поставить на колени.

И я по лестнице бегу,
Как будто выхожу впервые
На эти улицы в снегу
И вымершие мостовые.

Везде встают, огни, уют,
Пьют чай, торопятся к трамваям.
В теченье нескольких минут
Вид города неузнаваем.

В воротах вьюга вяжет сеть
Из густо падающих хлопьев,
И чтобы во-время поспеть,
Все мчатся недоев-недопив.

DAYBREAK

You meant all in my destiny once:
Then the war, the disaster, occurred,
And of you for a timeless long time
Not a rumour came through, not a word.

Now across the great length of these years
Comes your voice to disturb me again:
After reading your testament here
All the night, I awoke from my swoon.

My desire is to be among people,
And in crowds, in their bustle and ease:
I could shatter all things into fragments,
I could bring them all down to their knees.

And I run all the way down the stairs
Just as if I had never before
Come out into long empty pavements
And these wide streets enshrouded in snow.

There is homeliness, lights, everywhere,
People wake, drink their tea, rush for trams:
Till within a small matter of minutes
The whole face of the town has been changed;

And the blizzard is weaving a network
Of its swift falling snow on the gate;
But their food and their tea lie unfinished
As they hurry in case they are late.

Я чувствую за них за всех,
Как будто побывал в их шкуре,
Я таю сам, как тает снег,
Я сам, как утро, брови хмурю.

Со мною люди без имен,
Деревья, дети, домоседы.
Я ими всеми побежден,
И только в том моя победа.

Just as though I were under their skin
I can feel all their thoughts as my own,
And I melt with the melting of snow,
Like the morning my brows wear a frown.

For with me remain those without names,
The homely, and children, and trees:
In my utter conquest by them all
Is the sole of my victories.

ЧУДО

Он шел из Вифании в Ерусалим,
Заранее грустью предчувствий томим.

Колючий кустарник на круче был выжжен,
Над хижиной ближней не двигался дым,
Был воздух горяч и камыш неподвижен,
И Мертвого моря покой недвижим.

И в горечи, спорившей с горечью моря,
Он шел с небольшою толпой облаков
По пыльной дороге на чье-то подворье,
Шел в город на сборище учеников.

И так углубился он в мысли свои,
Что поле в унынье запахло полынью.
Всё стихло.   Один он стоял посредине,
А местность лежала пластом в забытьи.
Всё перемешалось: теплынь и пустыня,
И ящерицы, и ключи, и ручьи.

Смоковница высилась невдалеке,
Совсем без плодов, только ветки да листья.
И он ей сказал: «Для какой ты корысти?
Какая мне радость в твоем столбняке?

Я жажду и алчу, а ты — пустоцвет,
И встреча с тобой безотрадней гранита.
О, как ты обидна и недаровита!
Останься такой до скончания лет».

THE MIRACLE

From Bethany towards Jerusalem
A sorrowful foreboding weighed on him.

The smoke stood moveless on the hut nearby,
The prickly shrubs lay scorched upon the hill,
The reeds were motionless, the air hung dry
And all the Dead Sea motionless and still.

In bitterness matched by the bitter Sea,
And one small crowd of clouds to follow him,
He walked the dusty road towards the town
Where his disciples waited at an inn.

But so profoundly was he lost in thought
That wormwood bitterness suffused the field
Till all grew still.   He stood alone.   And round
Him lay the landscape, drowsy as a sheet,
In which all things became confused: the springs
And streams, the lizards, desert and the heat.

Beside him stood a fig-tree bare of fruit
Upon which only leaves and branches grew;
He turned to it: 'What profit do you bring?
From such dead wood what joy have I of you?

'I hunger and I thirst: but you're sterile
And comfortless as granite in your ways:
Why, for your failure and your uselessness
May you remain like this through all your days!'

По дереву дрожь осужденья прошла,
Как молнии искра по громоотводу,
Смоковницу испепелило до тла.

Найдись в это время минута свободы
У листьев, ветвей, и корней, и ствола,
Успели б вмешаться законы природы.
Но чудо есть чудо, и чудо есть Бог.
Когда мы в смятенье, тогда средь разброда
Оно настигает мгновенно, врасплох.

A tremor coursed in doom down through the tree
As lightning strikes upon a lightning-rod,
And levelled it to ashes instantly.

Had but a moment's freedom charged the heart
Of trunk and roots, of branches and of leaves,
The laws of nature would have played their part;
But miracles are miracles, are God:
And when we are dismayed, when most we stray,
They suddenly surprise us in the way.

ЗЕМЛЯ

В московские особняки
Врывается весна нахрапом.
Выпархивает моль за шкапом
И ползает по летним шляпам,
И прячут шубы в сундуки.

По деревянным антресолям
Стоят цветочные горшки
С левкоем и желтофиолем,
И дышат комнаты привольем,
И пахнут пылью чердаки.

И улица за панибрата
С оконницей подслеповатой,
И белой ночи и закату
Не разминуться у реки.

И можно слышать в коридоре
Что происходит на просторе,
О чем в случайном разговоре
С капелью говорит апрель.
Он знает тысячи историй
Про человеческое горе,
И по заборам стынут зори,
И тянут эту канитель.

И та же смесь огня и жути
На воле и в жилом уюте,
И всюду воздух сам не свой.
И тех же верб сквозные прутья,
И тех же белых почек вздутья
И на окне, и на распутье,
На улице и в мастерской.

THE EARTH

Spring into each Moscow house
Bursts with its impertinence;
Moths behind the dresser rise
Crawling on the summer hats;
Fur coats are secreted in trunks.

In the wooden upper storey
Stock and wallflower blossoms dress
Pots upon the window sill
And the rooms breathe ampleness,
The attic blows its dusty smell.

And the street strikes up a friendship
With the window's bleary eye
Nor can the river try to part
Where white night and sunset lie.

Within the corridor you hear
What is taking place outside
And what casual gossip April
With the dripping thaw has vied:
How he knows a thousand stories
Of man's burden of travail . . .
Along the fences twilights chill
As they help unwind the tale.

And mingled fire and disquiet
Pervades the open and the home
And everywhere the air's unquiet;
The selfsame pussy-willow twigs,
The selfsame swelling white buds meet
In the window, at the crossroads,
And in the workshop and the street.

Зачем же плачет даль в тумане,
И горько пахнет перегной?
На то ведь и мое призванье,
Чтоб не скучали расстоянья,
Чтобы за городскою гранью
Земле не тосковать одной.

Для этого весною ранней
Со мною сходятся друзья,
И наши вечера — прощанья,
Пирушки наши — завещанья,
Чтоб тайная струя страданья
Согрела холод бытия.

Why then do far miles weep in mist?
Why does the dung reek bitterness?
Surely it is my vocation
To prevent the loneliness
Of distances, to keep the earth
Outside the town from desolation.

And so for this in early spring
My friends and I together meet,
And our evenings are departings,
And all our parties testaments,
That a hidden stream of suffering
May warm the coldness of existence.

ДУРНЫЕ ДНИ

Когда на последней неделе
Входил он в Иерусалим,
Осанны навстречу гремели,
Бежали с ветвями за ним.

А дни всё грозней и суровей,
Любовью не тронуть сердец,
Презрительно сдвинуты брови,
И вот послесловье, конец.

Свинцовою тяжестью всею
Легли на дворы небеса.
Искали улик фарисеи,
Юля перед ним, как лиса.

И темными силами храма
Он отдан подонкам на суд,
И с пылкостью тою же самой,
Как славили прежде, клянут.

Толпа на соседнем участке
Заглядывала из ворот,
Толклись в ожиданье развязки
И тыкались взад и вперед.

И полз шопоток по соседству
И слухи со многих сторон.
И бегство в Египет и детство
Уже вспоминались, как сон.

EVIL DAYS

When in that last and final week
He came into Jerusalem
The loud hosannas thundered up
And crowds with branches followed him.

Each day more terrible and grim,
Cold hearts that love would not unbend,
The eyebrows raised contemptuously,—
And now the epilogue, the end.

The skies with their whole leaden weight
Lay pressing on the roof-tops' line:
Like foxes fawning over him
The Pharisees sought for a sign.

And when the temple's darkened powers
Gave him for judgment to the crowd,
Once they had praised him fervently
But now their curses rang out loud.

The mob that thronged outside the gates
Kept gazing in expectantly
And, waiting for the end to come,
Shoved back and forth impatiently,

While whispers crawled about the place
And rumours crept along the ways.
But he remembered like a dream
The Egypt road, his childhood days;

Припомнился скат величавый
В пустыне, и та крутизна,
С которой всемирной державой
Его соблазнял сатана.

И брачное пиршество в Кане,
И чуду дивящийся стол,
И море, которым в тумане
Он к лодке, как по суху, шел.

И сборище бедных в лачуге,
И спуск со свечою в подвал,
Где вдруг она гасла в испуге,
Когда воскрешенный вставал . . .

Recalling the majestic mount
Within the desert, and that height
From whose peak Satan tempted him
With thoughts of universal might;

And, at the Cana marriage feast,
Their wonder at the miracle;
The sea which he walked on like land
Towards the boat as deep mist fell;

The beggarly crowd in the hovel,
The cellar down which he was led,
The candle gutting out in fear
When Lazarus rose from the dead . . .

МАГДАЛИНА

I

Чуть ночь, мой демон тут как тут,
За прошлое моя расплата.
Придут и сердце мне сосут
Воспоминания разврата,
Когда, раба мужских причуд,
Была я дурой бесноватой
И улицей был мой приют.

Осталось несколько минут,
И тишь наступит гробовая.
Но раньше, чем они пройдут,
Я жизнь свою, дойдя до края,
Как алавастровый сосуд,
Перед тобою разбиваю.

О, где бы я теперь была,
Учитель мой и мой Спаситель,
Когда б ночами у стола
Меня бы вечность не ждала,
Как новый, в сети ремесла
Мной завлеченный посетитель.

Но объясни, что значит грех
И смерть и ад, и пламень серный,
Когда я на глазах у всех
С тобой, как с деревом побег,
Срослась в своей тоске безмерной.

Когда твои стопы, Исус,
Оперши о свои колени,
Я, может, обнимать учусь
Креста четырехгранный брус
И, чувств лишаясь, к телу рвусь,
Тебя готовя к погребенью.

MARY MAGDALEN

I

With nightfall my familiar comes,
The reckoning I owe my past,
And then my heart is gnawed within
By recollections of my lust,
The days when I was prey to men,
A fool senseless and indiscreet
Whose only haunt was in the street.

And just a few moments remain—
Then comes the silence of the tomb.
But now before the minutes take
Me, here upon the final brink,
My life before you I would break,
An alabaster vase of doom.

For, oh, my teacher and my Saviour,
Just where and what now would I be
Did not waiting eternity
Approach my table each nightfall
As though another client fell
Into the meshes of my guile?

But tell me simply what sin means,—
What death, and hell, and brimstone flame?—
When I, as everyone can see,
In boundless sorrow one and same
Grow into you, graft on a tree;

And, Jesus, when I hold you fast,
Your feet upon my bending knees,
Perhaps I'm learning to embrace
The rough cross with its four-square beam,
And swoon to strain your body close
And to prepare you for the tomb.

МАГДАЛИНА

II

У людей пред праздником уборка.
В стороне от этой толчеи
Обмываю миром из ведерка
Я стопы пречистые твои.

Шарю и не нахожу сандалий.
Ничего не вижу из-за слез.
На глаза мне пеленой упали
Пряди распустившихся волос.

Ноги я твои в подол уперла,
Их слезами облила.   Исус,
Ниткой бус их обмотала с горла,
В волосы зарыла, как в бурнус.

Будущее вижу так подробно,
Словно ты его остановил.
Я сейчас предсказывать способна
Вещим ясновиденьем сивилл.

Завтра упадет завеса в храме,
Мы в кружок собьемся в стороне,
И земля качнется под ногами,
Может быть, из жалости ко мне.

Перестроятся ряды конвоя,
И начнется всадников разъезд.
Словно в бурю смерч, над головою
Будет к небу рваться этот крест.

MARY MAGDALEN

II

Spring-cleaning comes before the Feast:
Out from the crowd's press I retreat
And with my little pail of myrrh
I bend to wash your most pure feet.

My groping hands search for the sandals
But tears come blinding, and I fail;
The loosened strands of flowing hair
Obscure my eyes as with a veil.

I've placed your feet upon my skirt,
Jesus; with tears I've watered them;
And wrapped round them my string of beads:
My hair hangs cloak-like over them.

As if you'd stopped its course, the future
In its detail I can descry:
A Sibyl's prescience lies on me
Who can this moment prophesy:

Tomorrow the temple veil will cleave
While we crouch huddled, helplessly;
The earth will heave under our feet,
As though with sympathy for me;

The guards will fall into their ranks,
The horsemen break up and ride by;
A whirlwind in the storm, the cross
Will tear above into the sky.

Брошусь на землю у ног распятья,
Обомру и закушу уста.
Слишком многим руки для объятья
Ты раскинешь по концам креста.

Для кого на свете столько шири,
Столько муки и такая мощь?
Есть ли столько душ и жизней в мире?
Столько поселений, рек и рощ?

Но пройдут такие трое суток
И столкнут в такую пустоту,
Что за этот страшный промежуток
Я до воскресенья дорасту.

I'll fall before it to the earth,
Benumbed, with anguish on my face:
While your arms outstretched on the cross
Spread too wide with your vast embrace;

For who in all the world needs this
Embrace, such torment and such power?
Has earth so many lives and souls,
Woods, rivers, villages, to shew?

And yet those three days will pass by,
But crush me in so deep a night
In that dread interval I'll grow
Into the Resurrection's height!

ГЕФСИМАНСКИЙ САД

Мерцаньем звезд далеких безразлично
Был поворот дороги озарен.
Дорога шла вокруг горы Масличной,
Внизу под нею протекал Кедрон.

Лужайка обрывалась с половины.
За нею начинался Млечный путь.
Седые серебристые маслины
Пытались вдаль по воздуху шагнуть.

В конце был чей-то сад, надел земельный.
Учеников оставив за стеной,
Он им сказал: «Душа скорбит смертельно,
Побудьте здесь и бодрствуйте со мной».

Он отказался без противоборства,
Как от вещей, полученных взаймы,
От всемогущества и чудотворства,
И был теперь, как смертные, как мы.

Ночная даль теперь казалась краем
Уничтоженья и небытия.
Простор вселенной был необитаем,
И только сад был местом для житья.

И, глядя в эти черные провалы,
Пустые, без начала и конца,
Чтоб эта чаша смерти миновала,
В поту кровавом он молил отца.

Смягчив молитвой смертную истому,
Он вышел за ограду.   На земле
Ученики, осиленные дремой,
Валялись в придорожном ковыле.

GETHSEMANE

The placid glimmering of distant stars
Illumined the wide turning of the road
That circled round the Mount of Olivet:
Below its quietness the Kedron flowed.

A field of grass melted away to where,
Beyond, the Milky Way began its flare:
Hoary and silver-headed olive trees
Tried in the distance to tread through the air.

Close by them an allotment garden lay.
He turned to his disciples quietly:
'My soul is stricken by a deathly sorrow,
Remain outside and keep the watch with me.'

How unresistingly relinquishing
(Like idle things borrowed upon the hour)
Omnipotence and power of miracles,
Became he then as mortal as we are!

And night's dark depths assumed the features of
Annihilation's brink, and nothingness;
The world seemed uninhabitable then,
And only in the garden lay life's place.

And as he gazed into the black abyss
Of unbeginning, endless, emptiness,
He prayed his Father through a sweat of blood
This cup of death pass from before his face.

His agony assuaged by that long prayer,
He went back through the garden and he found
All his disciples overcome by sleep
And slumped across the grass verge on the ground;

Он разбудил их: «Вас господь сподобил
Жить в дни мои, вы ж разлеглись, как пласт.
Час сына человеческого пробил.
Он в руки грешников себя предаст».

И лишь сказал, неведомо откуда
Толпа рабов и скопище бродяг.
Огни, мечи и впереди — Иуда
С предательским лобзаньем на устах.

Петр дал мечом отпор головорезам
И ухо одному из них отсек.
Но слышит: «Спор нельзя решать железом,
Вложи свой меч на место, человек.

Неужто тьмы крылатых легионов
Отец не снарядил бы мне сюда?
И, волоска тогда на мне не тронув,
Враги рассеялись бы без следа.

Но книга жизни подошла к странице,
Которая дороже всех святынь.
Сейчас должно написанное сбыться,
Пускай же сбудется оно.   Аминь.

Ты видишь, ход веков подобен притче
И может загореться на ходу.
Во имя страшного ее величья
Я в добровольных муках в гроб сойду.

Я в гроб сойду и в третий день восстану,
И, как сплавляют по реке плоты,
Ко мне на суд, как баржи каравана,
Столетья поплывут из темноты».

But wakened them: 'To you God granted life
Within my days, yet you sprawl sluggards still!
Now strikes the hour set for the Son of Man
When he shall suffer under sinners' will.'

Almost at once out of the dark nowhere
Swarmed in a crowd of thieves and nondescripts
With torches and with blades,—and at their head
Came Judas, with the false kiss on his lips.

When Peter held the murderers off by force
And struck off one of their ears with his sword,
'Steel cannot settle any arguments:
So sheathe your sword again,' was what he heard.

'Think you my Father could not send his hosts
Of legioned angels to my side to fight?
No hair upon my head would then be touched,
My enemies would scatter out of sight.

'But now the book of life has reached one page
More precious than all most-enhallowed things:
What has been written must now be fulfilled:
Amen. Amen to what the future brings.

'For, see, the ages like a parable
March on until they burst aflame and burn,
And in the name of their dread majesty
Through voluntary torment I'll go down

'Into the grave. But on the third day rise;
And then like rafts that float down-river dumb,
Like trains of barges, to my judgment seat
Out of the night the centuries will come!'

II

WHEN THE SKIES CLEAR

КОГДА РАЗГУЛЯЕТСЯ

_____ *

Во всем мне хочется дойти
До самой сути:
В работе, в поисках пути,
В сердечной смуте.

До сущности протекших дней,
До их причины,
До оснований, до корней,
До сердцевины.

Все время схватывая нить
Судеб, событий,
Жить, думать, чувствовать, любить,
Свершать открытья.

О, если бы я только мог,
Хотя отчасти,
Я написал бы восемь строк
О свойствах страсти!

О беззаконьях, о грехах,
Бегах, погонях,
Нечаянностях впопыхах,
Локтях, ладонях.

Я вывел бы ее закон,
Ее начало,
И повторял ее имен
Инициалы.

* Pasternak gave no title to this poem. See also p. 104.

IN ALL MY WAYS

In all my ways let me pierce through
Into the very essence,
At work, or following my path,
Or in heartfelt perturbance;

Straight to the soul of days now gone,
The source from which they flow,
To their foundations, to their roots
And to their very core;

Always and still grasping the thread
Of fate and acts, thereby
To live, to think, to feel, to love
And blaze discovery.

Oh, that I only had the power,
Even after a fashion,
Then were there eight lines I would write
On properties of passion!

And on iniquities and sins,
On flights and on alarms,
On errors made in sudden haste,
On elbows and on palms!

So passion's law I would portray,
The source from which she came,
And carefully I would rehearse
The letters of her name,

Я б разбивал стихи как сад.
Всей дрожью жилок
Цвели бы липы в них подряд —
Гуськом, в затылок.

В стихи б я внес дыханье роз,
Дыханье мяты,
Луга, осоку, сенокос,
Грозы раскаты.

Так некогда Шопен вложил
Живое чудо
Фольварков, парков, рощ, могил
В свои этюды.

Достигнутого торжества
Игра и мука —
Натянутая тетива
Тугого лука.

And like a garden set my rhymes:
Within it on the hour
The trembling lindens row by row
Would one by one break flower!

My verse would know the roses' scent
And mint would fill the air;
The meadows, sedge, the harvest hay,
The thunder, would breathe there;

As once when Chopin interfused
The living miracle
Of farms and parks and tombs and glades
Within his *Etudes'* spell.

Oh, how the play, the suffering
Of triumph once attained
Is like the pressure of a bow
On which the string is strained!

Быть знаменитым — некрасиво.
Не это подымает ввысь.
Не надо заводить архива,
Над рукописями трястись.

Цель творчества — самоотдача,
А не шумиха, не успех.
Позорно, ничего не знача,
Быть притчей на устах у всех.

Но надо жить без самозванства,
Так жить, чтобы в конце концов
Привлечь к себе любовь пространства,
Услышать будущего зов.

И надо оставлять пробелы
В судьбе, а не среди бумаг,
Места и главы жизни целой
Отчеркивая на полях.

И окунаться в неизвестность
И прятать в ней свои шаги,
Как прячется в тумане местность,
Когда в нем не видать ни зги.

Другие по живому следу
Пройдут твой путь за пядью пядь,
Но пораженья от победы
Ты сам не должен отличать.

И должен ни единой долькой
Не отступаться от лица,
Но быть живым, живым и только
Живым и только до конца.

IT'S UNBECOMING

It's unbecoming to have fame
For this is not what elevates,
And there's no need to keep archives
Or dote over your manuscripts;

Creation's way is—to give all,
And not to bluster or eclipse:
How mean, when you don't signify,
To be on everybody's lips!

But life must be without pretence;
Conduct your days that finally
You may indraw far-distant love
And hear the call of years to be.

And gaps you leave must not be found
Amid your papers, but in fate:
A whole life's chapters and contents
You may correct or annotate.

Plunge then into obscurity,
Concealing in it every pace
Just as the landscape disappears
Into the fog, and leaves no trace.

For others on the living trail
Will step by step pursue your way,
Yet you yourself must not discern
What is defeat, what victory:

And never for a single instant
Betray your true self, or pretend,
But be alive, and only living,
And only living to the end.

ДУША

Душа моя, печальница
О всех в кругу моем,
Ты стала усыпальницей
Замученных живьем.

Тела их бальзамируя,
Им посвящая стих,
Рыдающею лирою
Оплакивая их,

Ты в наше время шкурное
За совесть и за страх
Стоишь могильной урною,
Покоящей их прах.

Их муки совокупные
Тебя склонили ниц.
Ты пахнешь пылью трупною
Мертвецких и гробниц.

Душа моя, скудельница,
Все, виденное здесь,
Перемолов, как мельница,
Ты превратила в смесь.

И дальше перемалывай
Все бывшее со мной,
Как сорок лет без малого,
В погостный перегной.

MY SOUL

My soul, who still keep grieving
On all surrounding me,
You are a sepulchre to these
Who died in agony.

Your balm is on their corpses,
Theirs is your muted hymn,
Your tears hang on the lyre
Now mourning over them;

And, in our selfish age,
For honour and for awe
Are you become a burial-urn
To ease their ashes' sore;

Their agonies conspire
To crush you to earth's gloom,
You bear the smell of their dust round
In mortuary and tomb.

My soul, who are my charnel-house,
All that we here may keep
Of grist you gather like a mill
And crush it to a heap:

But grind, oh, keep on grinding
All that composed my past,
Like these scarce forty years gone by,
Into the grave's compost.

ЕВА

Стоят деревья у воды,
И полдень с берега крутого
Закинул облака в пруды,
Как переметы рыболова.

Как невод, тонет небосвод,
И в это небо, точно в сети
Толпа купальщиков плывет,
Мужчины, женщины и дети.

Пять-шесть купальщиц в лозняке
Выходят на берег без шума
И выжимают на песке
Свои купальные костюмы.

И, на подобие ужей,
Ползут и вьются кольца пряжи,
Как будто искуситель-змей
Скрывался в мокром трикотаже.

О, женщина, твой вид и взгляд
Ничуть меня в тупик не ставят.
Ты вся, как горла перехват,
Когда его волненье сдавит.

Ты создана как бы вчерне,
Как строчка из другого цикла,
Как будто не шутя во сне
Из моего ребра возникла.

И тотчас вырвалась из рук
И выскользнула из объятья,
Сама смятенье и испуг
И сердца мужеского сжатье.

EVE

Trees rise along the waterside
And from the hill the summer day
Casts clouds into the shining pools,
Like fisher-nets that teem with prey;

Where like a seine the sky sinks down
Into this heaven-net array
A shoal of bathers splash and swim
As women, men and children play.

About six women from the willows
Run noiseless to the beach, and stand
And wring out their wet bathing suits
Upon the long line of the sand,

Till almost like grass snakes the coils
Of their costumes twist round and wind
As though the Tempter-snake himself
Had used the folds to hide behind.

Yet, woman, though you gaze on me
How little you perplex my heart!
You're merely like a lump that swells
When swift emotion chokes my throat.

Your fashioning was somewhat rough,
Like verse awry within a poem,
As though you actually had sprung
Out of my side during a dream

And torn yourself out of my arms,
From my embrace slipping apart,—
Who are the very fear, dismay,
And dread confusion of man's heart!

БЕЗ НАЗВАНИЯ

Недотрога, тихоня в быту,
Ты сейчас вся огонь, вся — горенье.
Дай, запру я твою красоту
В темном тереме стихотворенья.

Посмотри, как преображена
Огневой кожурой абажура
Конура, край стены, край окна,
Наши тени и наши фигуры.

Ты с ногами сидишь на тахте,
Под себя их поджав по-турецки.
Все равно, на свету, в темноте —
Ты всегда рассуждаешь по-детски.

За беседой ты нижешь на шнур
Горсть на платье скатившихся бусин.
Слишком грустен твой вид, чересчур
Разговор твой прямой безыскусен.

Пошло слово «любовь», ты права;
Я придумаю кличку иную.
Для тебя я весь мир, все слова,
Если хочешь, переименую.

Разве хмурый твой вид передаст
Чувств твоих рудоносную залежь,
Сердца тайно светящийся пласт?
Для чего же глаза ты печалишь?

NO NAME

Who are so difficult and so demure,
Now you are all afire, wholly flame:
Let me then take your beauty and immure
It in the attic of a poem's frame.

Yet see how strangely different have grown
The corners of the wall, the window's edges—
Outside the lampshade's fiery skin are thrown
Our shadows and our darkened images.

And there, your legs beneath you, like a Turk
You sit upon the sofa, night-beguiled:
No matter whether in the light or dark
You always argue like a little child,

And while we talk you thread upon a string
A pile of beads that scattered to the floor;
Your eyes are sad, too sad for anything,
Your conversation too naïve by far.

But this word 'love', you're right, is trivial too:
I shall invent some name much better still;
For you I shall re-name the world, for you
All words that are, if such should be your will.

Yet do you think your sad glance will impart
The ore-streams whence your hidden feelings rise,
The shining secret ore-streams of your heart?
Then wherefore comes this grieving to your eyes?

ПЕРЕМЕНА

Я льнул когда-то к беднякам —
Не из возвышенного взгляда,
А потому, что только там
Шла жизнь без помпы и парада.

Хотя я с барством был знаком
И с публикою деликатной,
Я дармоедству был врагом
И другом голи перекатной.

И я старался дружбу свесть
С людьми из трудового званья,
За что и делали мне честь,
Меня считая тоже рванью.

Был осязателен без фраз,
Вещественен, телесен, весок
Уклад подвалов без прикрас
И чердаков без занавесок.

И я испортился с тех пор,
Как времени коснулась порча,
И горе возвели в позор,
Мещан и оптимистов корча.

Всем тем, кому я доверял,
Я с давних пор уже неверен.
Я человека потерял,
С тех пор, как всеми он потерян.

THE CHANGE

I used to fawn once on the poor,
Not led by lofty sentiments
But simply for the fact that there
Life bore no pomp or circumstance.

And close though I was to the lordly
And to the genteel and refined,
Yet was I foe to parasites,
And to the vagrant poor, a friend.

I tried to win the love of men
Whose toil was their sole dignity
For which they granted me this honour:
As dregs they also counted me.

There was an unaffected strength,
Substantial, physical, among
Those days spent in ungilded cellars
And attics where no curtains hung.

But I have slipped into decline
Since over time decay's touch came,
And posing optimists and bourgeois
Have elevated grief to shame:

In all whom I once gave my trust
My faith has gone long past recall,
For I have utterly lost man
Since ever he was lost by all.

ВЕСНА В ЛЕСУ

Отчаянные холода
Задерживали таянье.
Весна позднее, чем всегда,
Но и зато нечаянней.

С утра амурится петух,
И нет прохода курице.
Сосна, оборотясь на юг,
Лицом на солнце жмурится.

Хотя и парит и печет,
Еще недели целые
Дороги сковывает лед
Корою почернелою.

В лесу еловый мусор, хлам,
И снегом все завалено.
Водою с солнцем пополам
Затоплены проталины.

И небо в тучах, как в пуху,
Над грязной вешней жижицей
Застряло в сучьях наверху
И от жары не движется.

SPRING IN THE WOODS

Now the cold and desperate days
Withhold the coming of the thaw
And spring thereby will be more late
But her advent surprise the more.

From morningtide the amorous cock
Cuts all escape off for the hen,
The pine looks round towards the south
And blinks its eyes against the sun.

The air may steam with heavy heat
But still the long, long weeks drag past
And still the roads are chained by ice
Into a hard and blackening crust.

Decaying cones bestrew the wood
And snow chokes up the broken ground,
Out in the sun the thawing pools
Lie in their water, are half-drowned;

And heaven blows with clouds like down:
Above the dirty wash of spring
It's caught in branches overhead
And can't move for perspiring.

ИЮЛЬ

По дому бродит привиденье.
Весь день шаги над головой.
На чердаке мелькают тени.
По дому бродит домовой.

Везде болтается некстати,
Мешается во все дела,
В халате крадется к кровати,
Срывает скатерть со стола.

Ног у порога не обтерши,
Вбегает в вихре сквозняка
И с занавеской, как с танцоршей,
Взвивается до потолка.

Кто этот баловник-невежа
И этот призрак и двойник?
Да это наш жилец приезжий,
Наш летний дачник-отпускник.

На весь его недолгий роздых
Мы целый дом ему сдаем.
Июль с грозой, июльский воздух
Снял комнаты у нас внаем.

Июль, таскающий в одеже
Пух одуванчиков, лопух.
Июль, домой сквозь окна вхожий,
Все громко говорящий вслух.

Степной нечесанный растрепа,
Пропахший липой и травой,
Ботвой и запахом укропа,
Июльский воздух луговой.

JULY

There is a ghost who haunts our home
And paces overhead all day
While shadows flitter through the attic:
A goblin's here to range and stray.

He'll fuss futilely everywhere
And interfere with all you do,
Creep in a dressing-gown to bed,
Or snatch the tablecloth from you;

Nor wipes his feet upon the mat,
But bursts in with a gusty whirl
And spins the curtain to the ceiling
As though it were a dancing-girl!

Who's this uncivil mischief-maker,
This two-faced ghost who dogs our ways?
He is our temporary lodger,
Here for his summer holidays.

We give the whole house up to him
Just for his momentary stay:
July of storms, air of July,
Has rented rooms with us today;

July, who scatters from his clothes
The fluff of dandelion spray,
July, who comes in through the window
And mutters loudly all the way;

His hair untidy and dishevelled,
But redolent of linden, rye,
Perfume of grass and beet and dill—
This meadow-sweet air of July.

ПО ГРИБЫ

Плетемся по грибы.
Шоссе. Леса. Канавы.
Дорожные столбы
Налево и направо.

С широкого шоссе
Идем во тьму лесную.
По щиколку в росе
Плутаем врассыпную.

А солнце под кусты
На грузди и волнушки
Чрез дебри темноты
Бросает свет с опушки.

Гриб прячется за пень.
На пень садится птица.
Нам вехой служит тень,
Чтобы с пути не сбиться.

Но время в сентябре
Отмерено так куцо,
Едва ль до нас заре
Сквозь чащу дотянуться.

Набиты кузовки,
Наполнены корзины,
Одни боровики
У доброй половины.

Уходим.   За спиной
Стеною лес недвижный,
Где день в красе земной
Сгорел скоропостижно.

MUSHROOMING

Where mushrooms grow we roam
By highway, ditch and wood
As to our left and right
Posts stand along the road,

And from the broad highway
Into the wood's dark view
We wander randomly,
Our ankles deep in dew;

While from the forest edge
Across this desert night
The sun creeps through the bush
To tint mushrooms with light.

A bird sits on the stump
Behind whose bulk they hide,
As we pursue our shadows
In case we turn aside.

But, in September, time
Is measured out so sparse,
The setting sun can scarce
Reach us across the grass.

Yet, now our packs are full
With all that we could find
And more than half we've plucked
Is only of one kind.

We leave the wood, which like
A wall stands movelessly,
Whence day's earth-loveliness
Has burnt out suddenly.

ТИШИНА

Пронизан солнцем лес насквозь.
Лучи стоят столбами пыли.
Отсюда, уверяют, лось
Выходит на дорог развилье.

В лесу молчанье, тишина,
Как будто жизнь в глухой лощине
Не солнцем заворожена,
А по совсем другой причине.

Действительно, невдалеке
Средь заросли стоит лосиха.
Пред ней деревья в столбняке.
Вот отчего в лесу так тихо.

Лосиха ест лесной подсед,
Хрустя, обгладывает молодь.
Задевши за ее хребет,
Болтается на ветке жолудь.

Иван-да-Марья, зверобой,
Ромашка, Иван-чай, татарник,
Опутанные ворожбой,
Глазеют, обступив кустарник.

Во всем лесу один ручей
В овраге, полном благозвучья,
Твердит то тише, то звончей
Про этот небывалый случай.

Звеня на всю лесную падь
И оглашая лесосеку
Он что-то хочет рассказать
Почти словами человека.

STILLNESS

The wood is riddled through with sun
Which pours down in dust-pillared rays,
And here, they say, the elk comes out
Into the forking of the ways.

Within the wood is silence, peace:
Life in the vale stills to a pause
As though spellbound, not by the sun
But for some other secret cause.

And, sure enough, not far away
A young elk stands where thickets press,
And trees, dumbstruck to look at her,
Fill all the wood with voicelessness.

She chews the tender forest green
And nibbles where the fresh shoots twine;
An acorn swinging on a twig
Keeps bumping gently on her spine.

Purple cow-wheat, gold Saint John's wort,
Rosebay, thistle, camomile—
As though enchanted by a spell
They gaze on her, and stare, and smile;

While through the forest one lone stream,
Its music filling the ravine,
Sings now in hushed, now ringing tones
Of this which it had never seen,

And drowns out the woodcutters' blows
As through the wood it peals its way:
In human, almost human, words
There's something that it longs to say!

СТОГА

Снуют пунцовые стрекозы,
Летят шмели во все концы.
Колхозницы смеются с возу,
Проходят с косами косцы.

Пока хорошая погода,
Гребут и ворошат корма
И складывают до захода
В стога, величиной с дома.

Стог принимает на закате
Вид постоялого двора,
Где ночь ложится на полати
В накошенные клевера.

К утру, когда потемки реже,
Стог высится, как сеновал,
В котором месяц мимоезжий,
Зарывшись, переночевал.

Чем свет — телега за телегой
Лугами катятся впотьмах.
Наставший день встает с ночлега
С трухой и сеном в волосах.

А в полдень вновь синеют выси.
Опять стога, как облака,
Опять, как водка на анисе,
Земля душиста и крепка.

HAYSTACKS

Swift through the air crimson dragonflies dart,
Bumble-bees hum as they fly on all sides,
Farm girls are laughing on top of the cart,
Reapers go past as they carry their scythes.

Now while the weather is burning with sun
Heaps of thick fodder are turned and raked loose
And gathered together till daylight is done
High in hayricks that are large as a house.

Until at sunset the stack almost seems
Strange as a memoried posting-inn where
Night settles down by the stove to her dreams,
Deep in the clover fresh-harvested there.

Morning at hand; and the half-dark withdraws:
Once more at dawn the stack looms in the light,
Gaunt as a barn where the moon on its course
Dug itself in and slept all through the night.

Wagon on wagon awake with the light,
Roll through the lingering dark meadow air;
Once more a new day arises from night,
Shaking the pale wisps of hay from its hair.

Once more by noontide the high hills seem blue,
Once more the haystacks, like clouds, spill along:
Aniseed vodka of odour breathes through
Pores of the earth that is fragrant and strong.

ЛИПОВАЯ АЛЛЕЯ

Ворота с полукруглой аркой.
Холмы, луга, леса, овсы.
В ограде мрак и холод парка
И дом невиданной красы.

Там липы в несколько обхватов
Справляют в сумраке аллей,
Вершины друг за друга спрятав,
Свой двухсотлетний юбилей.

Они смыкают сверху своды.
Внизу — лужайка и цветник,
Который правильные ходы
Пересекают напрямик.

Под липами, как в подземельи,
Ни светлой точки на песке,
И лишь отверстием туннеля
Светлеет выход вдалеке.

Но вот приходят дни цветенья,
И липы в поясе оград
Разбрасывают вместе с тенью
Неотразимый аромат.

Гуляющие в летних шляпах
Вдыхают, кто бы ни прошел,
Непостижимый этот запах,
Доступный пониманью пчел.

THE LINDEN AVENUE

A gateway with a girdling arch,
And woods, hills, corn, and meadowlands,
While in the cool and darkened park
A house of rarest beauty stands—

There, in the twilight avenues,
The thickset lindens warily
Conceal their heads behind each other
And hold their bicentenary.

Above, their arches press and meet;
Below, a flower-bed and lawn
Stretch out, and crossing over them
Straight paths are regularly drawn;

But, cave-like underneath the lindens,
The gravel paths receive no beams
Of light, and like a tunnel's mouth
Only the distant entrance gleams.

Yet all the trees within the walls
During these present days of bloom
Are scattering within their shade
An irresistible perfume,

And passers-by in summer-hats
Breathe in on paths by which they go
A fragrance quite inscrutable
That only bees would chance to know;

Он составляет в эти миги,
Когда он за сердце берет,
Предмет и содержанье книги,
А парк и клумбы — переплет.

На старом дереве громоздком,
Завешивая сверху дом,
Горят, закапанные воском,
Цветы, зажженные огнем.

Such fragrance as would, at this time,
To those it captures by the heart,
Be theme and substance of a book
Whose cover is the flowers, the park.

While, on the old and heavy tree
That drapes above the mansion's frame,
Afire with wax that drips from them
Burn flowers lit up by drops of flame.

КОГДА РАЗГУЛЯЕТСЯ

Большое озеро как блюдо.
За ним — скопленье облаков,
Нагроможденных белой грудой
Суровых горных ледников.

По мере смены освещенья
И лес меняет колорит.
То весь горит, то черной тенью
Насевшей копоти покрыт.

Когда в исходе дней дождливых
Меж туч проглянет синева,
Как небо празднично в прорывах,
Как торжества полна трава!

Стихает ветер, даль расчистив.
Разлито солнце по земле.
Просвечивает зелень листьев,
Как живопись в цветном стекле.

В церковной росписи оконниц
Так в вечность смотрят изнутри
В мерцающих венцах бессонниц
Святые, схимники, цари.

Как будто внутренность собора
Простор земли, и чрез окно
Далекий отголосок хора
Мне слышать иногда дано.

Природа, мир, тайник вселенной,
Я службу долгую твою,
Объятый дрожью сокровенной,
В слезах от счастья отстою.

WHEN THE SKIES CLEAR

The massive lake is like a bowl
Beyond whose curve the rising tiers
Of clouds lean on the snowy breast
Of bitter mountain glaciers;

And with each movement in the light
The colours of the forest range
From blazing flame to blackness as
The shadows fall like soot, and change.

Day's end will bring an open sky
And blue between the clouds that pass
As after rain triumphantly
We see the festiveness of grass;

And as the distance clears, the wind
Dies down, the sun-bathed earth is bright
With green leaves whose translucency
Is tinted-glass suffused with light.

While, standing in their stained-glass frames,
All these great saints, ascetics, Tsars,
Unsleeping, in bright crowns of splendour,
Look from within beyond the stars,

As though the spaciousness of earth
Were a cathedral through whose pane
I sometimes may be privileged
To hear a distant choir's refrain.

Nature and world, creation's heart—
I'll hear your long Mass all my years
For there's a trembling in my soul,
Bathed in the happiness of tears.

ХЛЕБ

Ты выводы копишь полвека,
Но их не заносишь в тетрадь,
И если ты сам не калека,
То должен был что-то понять.

Ты понял блаженство занятий,
Удачи закон и секрет.
Ты понял, что праздность — проклятье,
И счастья без подвига нет.

Что ждет алтарей, откровений,
Героев и богатырей
Дремучее царство растений,
Могучее царство зверей.

Что первым таким откровеньем
Остался в сцепленьи судеб
Прапращуром в дар поколеньям
Взращенный столетьями хлеб.

Что поле во ржи и пшенице
Не только зовет к молотьбе,
Но некогда эту страницу
Твой предок вписал о тебе.

Что это и есть его слово,
Его небывалый почин
Средь круговращенья земного,
Рождений, скорбей и кончин.

BREAD

Five full decades' experience
You've gleaned, yet noted nothing down:
Unless you're quite bereft of sense
There's something that you must have known.

You've learned of occupation's bliss,
The law and secret of success,
You've learned that sloth is just a curse,
Achievement makes for happiness;

That, waiting for apocalypse,
For altars, heroes, bogatyrs,
The powerful vegetable kingdom lies,
The mighty animal kingdom rears;

And that this first apocalypse,
Born in the fates' outwhirling thread
And sire-bequeathed to ageless lips,
Was grown through centuries—in bread.

And fields of wheat, and fields of rye,
Ask more than just the threshing-stage:
It was of you in times gone by
That your ancestor penned that page.

For this is his undoubted word,
Unparalleled the task he sets
Amid this daily round of earth
And all its births, and griefs, and deaths.

ОСЕННИЙ ЛЕС

Осенний лес заволосател.
В нем тень и сон и тишина.
Ни белка, ни сова, ни дятел
Его не будят ото сна.

И солнце по тропам осенним
В него входя на склоне дня,
Кругом косится с опасеньем,
Не скрыта ли в нем западня.

В нем топи, кочки и осины
И мхи и заросли ольхи,
И где-то за лесной трясиной
Поют в селенье петухи.

Петух свой окрик прогорланит,
И вот он вновь надолго смолк,
Как будто он раздумьем занят,
Какой в запевке этой толк.

Но где-то в дальнем закоулке
Прокукарекает сосед;
Как часовой из караулки
Петух откликнется в ответ.

Он отзовется словно эхо,
И вот, за петухом петух
Отметят глоткою, как вехой,
Восток и запад, север, юг.

По петушиной перекличке
Расступится к опушке лес
И вновь увидит с непривычки
Поля и даль и синь небес.

THE AUTUMN WOOD

The autumn wood, unshaven, lies
Where shade and sleep and silence teem
And where no squirrel or woodpecker
Or owl can wake it from its dream.

And when the sun walks autumn paths
Into the wood at fall of day,
He squints round apprehensively
Lest snares lie hidden in his way;

But only aspens, mounds, and swamps
And moss and alder clumps grow there,
And cocks are singing in a village
Beyond the woodland marsh somewhere.

The cock gives full vent to his cry
And then again falls silent long
As though he had begun to doubt
What meaning there was in his song.

But somewhere from his distant nook
Another cock in turn gives cry,
And like a sentry at the post
He trumpets out his own reply,

And like an echo his response
Makes all the cocks in their turn mouth
Their voices like signposts that stand
To east and west, to north and south;

Till, challenged by their clarion-call,
The forest with newborn surprise
Awakes, and stretches out to gaze
At fields, horizon, and blue skies.

ЗАМОРОЗКИ

Холодным утром солнце в дымке
Стоит столбом огня в дыму.
Я тоже, как на скверном снимке,
Совсем неотличим ему.

Пока оно из мглы не выйдет,
Блеснув за прудом на лугу,
Меня деревья плохо видят
На отдаленном берегу.

Прохожий узнается позже,
Чем он пройдет, нырнув в туман.
Мороз покрыт гусиной кожей,
И воздух лжив, как слой румян.

Идешь по инею дорожки,
Как по настилу из рогож.
Земле дышать ботвой картошки
И стынуть — больше невтерпеж.

AUTUMN FROSTS

As though it were a pillared flame in smoke
The morning sun stands in the foggy air:
I too, as in a half-blurred photograph,
Am so obscured it cannot see me there;

For, while it shimmers far beyond the lake
Upon the meadows and cannot emerge
Out of the mist, then even lakeside trees
Can barely see me on this farther verge.

A casual passer-by is recognized
Only when fog has swallowed his last trace
In cold that's covered with goose-pimpled skin
And air as false as make-up on a face.

Go, walk upon the hoar-frost on the roads
As though you trod upon a matted floor:
Yet earth, that breathes decaying beetroot leaves
And frosts, finds these more than it can endure.

НОЧНОЙ ВЕТЕР

Стихли песни и пьяный галдеж.
Завтра надо вставать спозаранок.
В избах гаснут огни.   Молодежь
Разошлась по домам с погулянок.

Только ветер бредет наугад
Все по той же заросшей тропинке,
По которой с толпою ребят
Во-свояси он шел с вечеринки.

Он за дверью поник головой.
Он не любит ночных катавасий.
Он бы кончить хотел мировой
В споре с ночью свои несогласья.

Перед ними — заборы садов.
Оба спорят, не могут уняться.
За разборами их неладов
На дороге деревья толпятся.

THE NIGHT WIND

Tonight the songs and drunken brawls have died:
Tomorrow we must rise at break of day;
The fires in the izbas fall: outside
Men leave their drinks and take their homeward way.

And just the wind is left behind to roam
At random on the path by which today
He took a crowd of little children home
From their tea-party and their evening play;

He droops his head and hides behind a door
For fear of complications with the night
Whom he would rather now conciliate
To end their disagreements and their fight:

But garden fences rise up in their way;
They quarrel and they cannot make their peace:
Behind the frenzy of their argument
Crowds down the road an audience of trees.

ЗОЛОТАЯ ОСЕНЬ

Осень.   Сказочный чертог,
Всем открытый для обзора.
Просеки лесных дорог,
Заглядевшихся в озера.

Как на выставке картин:
Залы, залы, залы, залы
Вязов, ясеней, осин,
В позолоте небывалой.

Липы обруч золотой
Как венец на новобрачной;
Лик березы под фатой,
Подвенечной и прозрачной.

Погребенная земля
Под листвой в канавах, ямах.
В желтых кленах флигеля,
Словно в золоченых рамах.

Где деревья в сентябре
На заре стоят попарно,
И закат на их коре
Оставляет след янтарный;

Где нельзя ступить в овраг,
Чтоб не стало всем известно —
Так бушует, что ни шаг,
Под ногами лист древесный;

GOLDEN AUTUMN

The autumn is a faery hall
Thrown open to the world's inspection
Where vistaed avenues of trees
Gaze in the lakes at their reflection

As though at some picture display:
Here endless halls and halls unfold
And elms and ash and aspens grow
In an unprecedented gold.

And how the golden linden's band
Is like the garland on a bride!
The birch's face beneath its veil,
How limpid in her nuptial pride!

Now earth is buried deep away
In ditches where dry leaves are rolled
While houses stand in yellow maple
As though in picture frames of gold:

And when the trees stand two by two
Bathed in the sunrise in September,
Or when the sunset on their boughs
Leaves after it a trace of amber;

And when you step into no ditch
Without someone being bound to know
How much the rustle underfoot
Of leaves shews where you wish to go;

Где звучит в конце аллей
Эхо у крутого спуска,
И зари вишневый клей
Застывает в виде сгустка.

Осень.   Древний уголок
Старых книг, одеж, оружья,
Где сокровищ каталог
Перелистывает стужа.

And when the steep slope's echo rings
Down to the ending of the road
And sunset, like red cherry gum,
Coagulates and turns to blood:

Then autumn's here—an ancient nook
Of books, clothes, guns, forgotten pleasures
With which the cold goes browsing through
Its happy catalogue of treasures.

НЕНАСТЬЕ

Дождь дороги заболотил.
Ветер режет их стекло.
Он платок срывает с ветел
И стрижет их наголо.

Листья шлепаются оземь.
Едут люди с похорон.
Потный трактор пашет озимь
В восемь дисковых борон.

Черной вспаханною зябью
Листья залетают в пруд
И по возмущенной ряби
Кораблями в ряд плывут.

Брызжет дождик через сито.
Крепнет холода напор.
Точно все стыдом покрыто,
Точно в осени — позор.

Точно срам и поруганье
В стаях листьев и ворон
И дожде и урагане,
Хлещущих со всех сторон.

WET WEATHER

The rain drives slush along the roads
And sharp winds shatter through their glass:
They tear the willows' headscarf free
And crop them naked as they pass.

Leaves plashing down into the mud.
Some graveside mourners driving by.
A rain-dewed tractor through the fields
Urges its eight-disked harrow by.

Over the dark and furrowed soil
Leaves drift into the pool's calm reach;
The startled ripples bear them as
Like ships they sail, each after each.

A hazy drizzle sifting down.
The bitter cold bears in apace.
Somehow all's veiled in infamy,
Somehow this autumn breathes—disgrace.

And there's ignominy and shame
In herded leaves, in flocks of crows,
In rain and in the hurricane
That whips in from all sides and blows.

ТРАВА И КАМНИ

С действительностью иллюзию,
С растительностью гранит
Так сблизили Польша и Грузия,
Что это обеих роднит.

Как будто весной в Благовещенье
Им милости возвещены
Землей в каждой каменной трещине,
Травой из под каждой стены.

И те обещанья подхвачены
Природой, трудами их рук,
Искусствами, всякою всячиной,
Развитьем ремесл и наук;

Побегами жизни и зелени,
Развалинами старины,
Землей в каждой мелкой расселине,
Травой из под каждой стены;

Следами усердья и праздности,
Беседою, бьющей ключем,
Речами про разные разности,
Пустой болтовней ни о чем;

Пшеницей в полях выше сажени,
Сходящейся над головой,
Землей в каждой каменной скважине,
Травой в половице кривой;

GRASS AND STONES

Illusion set against reality,
The living grasses and dead stone,
Have been so fused by Poland and by Georgia
That both lands seem alike as one.

As though, on spring's Annunciation day,
Upon them promises now fall
From earth in all her rocky crevices,
The grass from under every wall.

And these their promises are taken up
By Nature, labours of their hands,
By skill, by each and every industry,
By trade and science in these lands;

By living shoots of life and greenery,
By antique ruins stooped to fall,
By earth in all her minute cleavages,
The grass from under every wall;

By instances of zeal and slothfulness,
By converse spurring into flame,
By speeches over sundry differences,
By empty chatter void of aim;

By rich fields taller than two yards of wheat,
Ears meeting overhead to dream;
By earth in all her rocky openings
And grass in every flooring beam;

Душистой, густой повиликою,
Столетьями, вверх по кусту,
Обвившей былое великое
И будущего красоту;

Сиренью, двойными оттенками
Лиловых и белых кистей
Пестреющей между простенками
Осыпавшихся крепостей.

Где люди в родстве со стихиями,
Стихии в соседстве с людьми,
Земля в каждом каменном выеме,
Трава перед всеми дверьми.

Где с гордою лирой Мицкевича
Таинственно слился язык
Грузинских цариц и царевичей
Из девичьих и базилик.

By thick and fragrant flowering creepers
That rise through bush through centuries,
Entwining still the greatness of the past
And beauty that before it lies;

By lilac, by the twin-compelling shades
Of mauve and white flowered witnesses
Emerging brilliant between
The walls of crumbling fortresses.

Where men strike kinship with the elements,
Where elements are kin with men,
Earth there will be in every rocky groove,
Before all doors the grass springs then:

Where secretly is blended the clear tongue
Of Georgian queens and sons of Kings
In maidens' rooms and in basilicas
When the proud lyre of Mickiewicz sings.

НОЧЬ

Идет без проволочек
И тает ночь, пока
Над спящим миром летчик
Уходит в облака.

Он потонул в тумане,
Исчез в его струе,
Став крестиком на ткани
И меткой на белье.

Под ним ночные бары,
Чужие города,
Казармы, кочегары,
Вокзалы, поезда.

Всем корпусом на тучу
Ложится тень крыла.
Блуждают, сбившись в кучу,
Небесные тела.

И страшным, страшным креном
К другим каким-нибудь
Неведомым вселенным
Повернут млечный путь.

В пространствах беспредельных
Горят материки.
В подвалах и котельных
Не спят истопники.

NIGHT

The night comes unattended,
Secreting all away,
As over sleeping countries
An airman cleaves his way.

The swirling fog engulfs him,
He drowns within the dark,
A tiny cross on clothing,
A little laundry mark.

Night inns lie underneath him,
Unknown towns in the plains,
Barracks and gaunt stokers,
Dark stations and night trains.

Heavy on a rain-cloud
The shadow of a wing:
All huddled lost together
The stars are wandering;

And terrible, most fearful
There swings out far away
To unknown universes
The curving Milky Way.

Through unconfined expanses
Vast continents still burn:
In boiler-rooms and cellars
The stokers keep their turn.

В Париже из под крыши
Венера или Марс
Глядят, какой в афише
Объявлен новый фарс.

Кому-нибудь не спится
В прекрасном далеке
На крытом черепицей
Старинном чердаке.

Он смотрит на планету,
Как будто небосвод
Относится к предмету
Его ночных забот.

Не спи, не спи, работай,
Не прерывай труда,
Не спи, борись с дремотой,
Как летчик, как звезда.

Не спи, не спи, художник,
Не предавайся сну.
Ты — вечности заложник
У времени в плену.

Beneath the eaves in Paris
Peeps Venus or else Mars
To glance up at the poster
Announcing some new farce;

While in the lovely distance
Lies one who cannot sleep
Where in his ancient attic
The tiles their vigil keep.

He gazes at a planet
As though the heavens might
Yet condescend to settle
His worries of the night.

Don't sleep, don't sleep, keep working,
Don't cease work for one hour:
Don't sleep, fight off this drowsing,
Like airmen, like a star;

Don't sleep, oh don't sleep, artist:
Above your slumbers climb—
Eternity's proud hostage
And prisoner of time!

ВЕТЕР

(Четыре отрывка о Блоке)

I

Кому быть живым и хвалимым,
Кто должен быть мертв и хулим,
Известно у нас подхалимам
Влиятельным только одним.

Не знал бы никто, может статься,
В почетели Пушкин, иль нет,
Без докторских их диссертаций,
На все проливающих свет.

Но Блок, слава Богу, иная,
Иная, по счастью, статья.
Он к нам не спускался с Синая,
Нас не принимал в сыновья.

Прославленный не по программе
И вечный вне школ и систем,
Он не изготовлен руками
И нам не навязан никем.

THE WIND

Four fragments on Blok

I

Who should remain alive and praised,
Who should stay dead without renown—
Depends upon criteria
That powerful sycophants lay down;

And none, of course, would ever know
If Pushkin might have won his fame
Had not their learned dissertations
As yet illumined his great name.

But, God be praised, Blok is not thus:
In quite another race he runs;
No thunder brought him from Sinai,
He did not choose us as his sons.

Illustrious (not by some plan),
Eternal (beyond system's laws),
He is not moulded by men's hands
Nor bound to any special cause.

II

Он ветрен, как ветер.   Как ветер,
Шумевший в имении в дни,
Как там еще Филька-фалетер
Скакал в голове шестерни.

И жил еще дед-якобинец,
Кристальной души радикал,
От коего ни на мизинец
И ветренник внук не отстал.

Тот ветер, проникший под ребра
И в душу, в течение лет
Недоброю славой и доброй
Помянут в стихах и воспет.

Тот ветер повсюду.   Он — дома,
В деревьях, в деревне, в дожде
В поэзии третьего тома,
В «Двенадцати», в смерти, везде.

II

He's gusty as the wind: and as the wind
He storms throughout the old estate by day
As though the old postillion were still
Upon his six-team galloping away;

And his ancestral Jacobin still lived,
That radical of clear, incisive mind
In whose footsteps not by a single inch
Would his high-flying grandchild lag behind.

Beneath the ribs this wind still penetrates,
And to the soul; till with the long years' stream
A poem sings, a song now celebrates
His course with ill repute or with esteem.

This wind we know is everywhere—at home,
In trees and in the villages, in rain
Or in his poetry's third volume
Or in *The Twelve*, and then in death again.

Широко, широко, широко
Раскинулись речка и луг.
Пора сенокоса, толо́ка,
Страда, суматоха вокруг.
Косцам у речного протока
Заглядываться недосуг.
Косьба разохотила Блока,
Схватил косовище барчук.
Ежа чуть не ранил с наскоку,
Косой полоснул двух гадюк.

Но он не доделал урока.
Упреки: лентяй, лежебока!
О детство!   О школы морока!
О песни пололок и слуг!

А к вечеру туча с востока.
Обложены север и юг.
И ветер жестокий не к сроку
Влетает и режется вдруг
О косы косцов, об осоку,
Резучую гущу излук.

О детство!   О школы морока!
О песни пололок и слуг!
Широко, широко, широко
Раскинулись речка и луг.

III

Widely, widely, widely
Spread the meadow and the stream:
Together! now's hay-making,
The busy harvest team;
No time to stare at reapers
Along the riverside!
Blok loved once the scythe-handle,
The noble's son in pride
Almost wounded a hedgehog,
Slew vipers with the scythe.

His lessons left untended,
Reproaches followed strong.
O childhood! weary schooldays!
O humble servants' song!

At evening from the east
Come clouds, to north and south;
A wind, untimely, cruel,
Cuts on the scythe's sharp mouth,
Cuts thickets on the sedge where
The river winds about.

O childhood! weary schooldays!
O humble servants' song!
Widely, widely, widely
Flows the meadow stream along.

Зловещ горизонт и внезапен,
И в кровоподтеках заря,
Как след незаживших царапин
И кровь на ногах косаря.

Нет счета небесным порезам,
Предвестникам бурь и невзгод,
И пахнет водой и железом
И ржавчиной воздух болот.

В лесу, на дороге, в овраге,
В деревне или на селе
На тучах такие зигзаги
Сулят непогоду земле.

Когда ж над большою столицей
Край неба так ржав и багрян,
С державою что-то случится,
Постигнет страну ураган.

Блок на небе видел разводы.
Ему предвещал небосклон
Большую грозу, непогоду,
Великую бурю, циклон.

Блок ждал этой бури и встряски.
Ее огневые штрихи
Боязнью и жаждой развязки
Легли в его жизнь и стихи.

IV

The ominous horizon suddenly
Bursts out into a scarlet mass of bruises
And burns there like a freshly-opened scar,
A reaper's leg from which the blood still oozes.

There is no limit to celestial wounds
That bring the storm and turn fair hopes to dust;
Out in the marshes the unfriendly air
Smells thick of water, iron and of rust.

Be it in forest, road, or the ravine,
In hamlet or in village that you stand,
These zigzags riding on the massive clouds
Can promise no good weather for the land.

And at this time, above the capital
When red with rust the sky's edge wears a frown,
Something most terrible will strike the state,
A hurricane will hurl our country down.

Blok saw the portents written in the sky.
On his horizon he discerned the form
Of some great menace, of a gathering cloud,
A cyclone, grim fear of a mighty storm.

Blok waited for this storm and its upsurge.
Its deepest elements of active fire
Lay in his living, and his poetry—
Their last fulfilment being his dread desire.

ДОРОГА

То насыпью, то глубью лога,
То по прямой за поворот,
Змеится лентою дорога
Безостановочно вперед.

По всем законам перспективы
За придорожные поля
Бегут мощеные извивы,
Не слякотя и не пыля.

Вот путь перебежал плотину,
На пруд не посмотревши вбок,
Который выводок утиный
Переплывает поперек.

Вперед то под гору, то в гору
Бежит прямая магистраль,
Как разве только жизни впору
Все время рваться вверх и вдаль.

Чрез тысячи фантасмагорий
И местности и времена,
Через преграды и подспорья
Несется к цели и она.

А цель ее — в гостях и дома —
Все пережить и все пройти,
Как оживляют даль изломы
Мимоидущего пути.

THE ROAD

Along the bank and down the grove
Then cutting through around the bend
As though a ribbon winding past,
The road runs forward without end.

Obeying all perspective's laws,
Beyond the roadside fields and plain
There lengthen out swift tarmac coils
Untouched by dust or slushy rain;

They run across a little dyke
Without a sideward glance to see
How in the pond a brood of ducks
Swims on the ripples happily.

But forward up and down the hills
The straight highway pursues its course
As only life perhaps can do,
To tear ahead with ceaseless force;

For so through myriad fantasies,
Through nightmares, and through time and space,
Through hindrances and through supports,
Life to its goal must also race,

And still its aim—abroad, at home—
Is to endure and to survive,
Just as the road that's running by
To distant tracts, brings them alive!

В БОЛЬНИЦЕ

Стояли как перед витриной,
Почти запрудив тротуар.
Носилки втолкнули в машину,
В кабину вскочил санитар.

И скорая помощь, минуя
Панели, подъезды, зевак,
Сумятицу улиц ночную,
Нырнула огнями во мрак.

Милиция, улицы, лица
Мелькали в свету фонаря.
Покачивалась фельдшерица
Со склянкою нашатыря.

Шел дождь, и в приемном покое
Уныло шумел водосток,
Меж тем как строка за строкою
Марали опросный листок.

Его положили у входа.
Всё в корпусе было полно.
Разило парами иода,
И с улицы дуло в окно.

Окно обнимало квадратом
Часть сада и неба клочок.
К палатам, полам и халатам
Присматривался новичок.

IN HOSPITAL

As though thronging a window display
They blocked up the pavement and street
Till the stretcher was shoved in the van:
The driver then leapt to his seat

And the ambulance plunged swiftly past
The pavements and idlers, through night
And the streets in their turmoil and dark,
While piercing the gloom with its light,

In whose powerful beam there flashed by
Policemen and heads and the street
As the nurse with the sal-ammonia
Kept swaying on unsteady feet.

In the downpour of rain the pipes moaned
And hummed through the hospital room
As they scribbled words line after line
Upon the enquiry form.

Then they gave him a bed by the door
Because there was no other place
And though iodine hung in the air
The window brought fresh breeze a space.

In the square of the window was framed
A part of the garden and sky
But the newcomer gazed round the wards
And floors and the coats passing by;

Как вдруг из расспросов сиделки,
Покачивавшей головой,
Он понял, что из переделки
Едва ли он выйдет живой.

Тогда он взглянул благодарно
В окно, за которым стена
Была точно искрой пожарной
Из города озарена.

Там в зареве рдела застава
И, в отсвете города, клен
Отвешивал веткой корявой
Больному прощальный поклон.

«О, Господи, как совершенны
Дела Твои,» — думал больной, —
«Постели, и люди, и стены,
Ночь смерти и город ночной.

Я принял снотворного дозу
И плачу, платок теребя.
О, Боже, волнения слезы
Мешают мне видеть Тебя.

Мне сладко при свете неярком,
Чуть падающем на кровать,
Себя и свой жребий подарком
Бесценным Твоим сознавать.

Кончаясь в больничной постели,
Я чувствую рук Твоих жар.
Ты держишь меня, как изделье,
И прячешь, как перстень в футляр.»

Till suddenly, after her questions
He saw how the nurse shook her head
And realized what little hope
Of life was left him on this bed.

Then he gratefully looked up towards
The window through which there now came
Burning light on the wall as though sparks
Had blown from a town set aflame:

And the town lay there burning in sunset,
But where its reflected light fell
Bowed a kindly and old maple tree:
Its withered branch bade him farewell.

And the sick man's thoughts welled up: 'O God,
How perfect your works are, how right!
All these people, these beds and these walls,
This death-night, the town in the night!

But I've taken a sleeping-draught now,
I'm crying, quite lost what to do:
Yet you know how these tears of emotion
Prevent me from looking at you.

And how wonderful here in the half-light
That's falling just over my bed
Just to know that my life and my fate
Are gifts without price you have shed!

Though I'll die on this sick-bed of mine
Your warm hand I feel guide my way,
For you've made me and hold me and now
Like a gem you encase me away!'

165

МУЗЫКА

Дом высился, как каланча.
По тесной лестнице угольной
Несли рояль два силача,
Как колокол на колокольню.

Они тащили вверх рояль
Над ширью городского моря,
Как с заповедями скрижаль
На каменное плоскогорье.

И вот в гостиной инструмент,
И город в свисте, шуме, гаме,
Как под водой на дне легенд,
Внизу остался под ногами.

Жилец шестого этажа
На землю посмотрел с балкона,
Как бы ее в руках держа
И ею властвуя законно.

Вернувшись внутрь, он заиграл
Не чью-нибудь чужую пьесу,
Но собственную мысль, хорал,
Гуденье мессы, шелест леса.

Раскат импровизаций нес
Ночь, пламя, гром пожарных бочек,
Бульвар под ливнем, стук колес,
Жизнь улиц, участь одиночек.

MUSIC

The building lifted like a tower
Along whose narrow climbing stair
Two strong men dragged a piano's weight
As though they took a bell up there

Above the town's outspreading sea
Where now the piano stood alone—
A tablet of commandments laid
Upon a great plateau of stone;

And when they reached the living room
The town, its whistles, noise, and roar,
Lay far down underneath their feet,
A legend on the ocean floor.

But from his fifth-floor balcony
A lodger gazed down to survey
All earth as though held in his hands
Or subject to his rightful sway.

He went in, and began to play:
Not of another's fantasy,
But his own vision, a chorale,
The drone of Mass, a forest's sigh;

The peal of improvised refrains
Bore night and flame and thunder then:
A boulevard in the rain, and wheels,
The life of streets, the fate of men.

Так ночью, при свечах, взамен
Былой наивности нехитрой
Свой сон записывал Шопен
На черной выпилке пюпитра.

Или, опередивши мир
На поколения четыре,
По крышам городских квартир
Грозой гремел полет Валькирий.

Или консерваторский зал
При адском грохоте и треске
До слез Чайковский потрясал
Судьбой Паоло и Франчески.

Once thus at night, by candlelight
The old naïveté lost its gleam
When on the dark-wood music stand
Chopin wrote down his living dream:

Or once, four aeons ere their time,
The town's rooftops their presence knew
Where in the fury of the storm
A thunder of Valkyries flew;

Or when in the Conservatoire
Amid the crack and crash of Hell,
Tchaikovsky drew their tears who heard
How Paolo and Francesca fell.

ПОСЛЕ ПЕРЕРЫВА

Три месяца тому назад,
Лишь только первые метели
На наш незащищенный сад
С остервененьем налетели,

Прикинул тотчас я в уме,
Что я укроюсь, как затворник,
И что стихами о зиме
Пополню свой весенний сборник.

Но навалились пустяки
Горой, как снежные завалы.
Зима, расчетам вопреки,
Наполовину миновала.

Тогда я понял, почему
Она во время снегопада
Снежинками пронзая тьму,
Заглядывала в дом из сада.

Она шептала мне: «Спеши!»
Губами, белыми от стужи,
А я чинил карандаши,
Отшучиваясь неуклюже.

Пока под лампой у стола
Я медлил зимним утром ранним,
Зима явилась и ушла
Непонятым напоминаньем.

AFTER THE INTERLUDE

Three months ago there first
Came down the snowstorm's wrath
Which in its fury burst
On our poor gardened earth,

And brought into my mind
The hermit's cold desire
To hide, to write, and find,
In wintry verses, fire.

But like a hill of snow
My thoughts heaped nonsense on,
My plans had lost their glow
And winter was half done;

Then only did I know
Why winter in the storm
Had pierced the dark with snow
And peered into my home:

She whispered 'Hurry!' then,
Her lips were pale with frost;
But, playing with a pen
I dawdled, joked, and lost.

Early one winter morn
As I sat down to write,
Winter passed by, was gone,
Unwritten, in the night.

ПЕРВЫЙ СНЕГ

Снаружи вьюга мечется
И все заносит в лоск.
Засыпана газетчица,
И заметен киоск.

На нашей долгой бытности
Казалось нам не раз,
Что снег идет из скрытности
И для отвода глаз.

Утайщик нераскаянный, —
Под белой бахромой,
Как часто нас с окраины
Он разводил домой!

Все в белых хлопьях скроется
Залепит снегом взор,
На ощупь, как пропоица,
Проходит тень во двор.

Движения поспешные.
Наверное опять
Кому-то что-то грешное
Приходится скрывать.

Повалит снег — и в трепете
Окно и частокол,
Но петель не расцепите,
Которые он сплел.

THE FIRST SNOW

Outside, the blizzard spins awhirl
To lay its coat on all,
And overwhelm the paper girl
And cover up her stall:

But often long experience
Has made us realize
That snow falls out of some pretence
Just to deceive our eyes;

And, uncontritely hiding you
Beneath white-tasselled snow,
How often from the outskirts has
He led you home once more!

Now everything is flaked with white,
Snow-blinded are our eyes:
A shadow gropes towards a door
As though in drunkenness,

And hurriedly then goes inside;
Oh, surely you can feel
There's something sinful that someone
Is anxious to conceal!

The snow is spreading—and alarms
Window and palisade,
But you will never yet unwind
The pattern it has made!

СНЕГ ИДЕТ

Снег идет, снег идет.
К белым звездочкам в буране
Тянутся цветы герани
За оконный переплет.

Снег идет, и все в смятеньи,
Все пускается в полет.
Черной лестницы ступени,
Перекрестка поворот.

Снег идет, снег идет,
Словно падают не хлопья,
А в заплатанном салопе
Сходит наземь небосвод.

Словно с видом чудака,
С верхней лестничной площадки,
Крадучись, играя в прятки,
Сходит небо с чердака.

Потому что жизнь не ждет,
Не оглянешься, и — святки.
Только промежуток краткий,
Смотришь, там и Новый Год.

Снег идет, густой — густой.
В ногу с ним, стопами теми,
В том же темпе, с ленью той
Или с той же быстротой
Может быть, проходит время?
Может быть, за годом год
Следуют, как снег идет,
Или как слова в поэме?

SNOW IS FALLING

Snow is falling, snow is falling:
Stretching to the window pane
Pale geraniums gaze out
Where the starflakes blow white rain.

Snow is falling, all's a flurry,
Everything wings off and flies:
Steps down in the shadowed staircase,
Corner where the crossroads rise.

Snow is falling, snow is falling—
Somehow, though, not flakes teem round
But heaven's arch, in ragged furs,
Is descending to the ground.

Looking like an old eccentric,
From the upper landing sly—
Creeping, playing at hide-and-seek—
From its attic steals the sky.

Flow of life is not for waiting;
Eyelid's wink, Christmas is here:
Just a moment, time's brief passing,
Look around and it's New Year.

Snow is falling, faster, faster:
Stepping out, in rhythmic feet,
Tempo same and same the drag,
Might not with the selfsame beat
Time itself flit by and pass?
Might not all years come and go
Like the words knit in a poem,
Like the falling of the snow?

Снег идет, снег идет,
Снег идет, и все в смятенье —
Убеленный пешеход,
Удивленные растенья,
Перекрестка поворот.

Snow is falling, snow is falling,
Snow is falling, all's a flurry—
Whitened walker in a hurry,
Flowers covered with surprise,
Corners where the crossroads rise.

СЛЕДЫ НА СНЕГУ

Полями наискось к закату
Уходят девушек следы.
Они их валенками вмяты
От слободы до слободы.

А вот ребенок жался к мамке.
Луч солнца, как лимонный морс,
Затек во впадины и ямки
И лужей света в льдину вмерз.

Он стынет вытекшею жижей
Яйца в разбитой скорлупе,
И синей линиею лыжи
Его срезают по тропе.

Луна скользит блином в сметане,
Все время скатываясь вбок.
За ней бегут вдогонку сани,
Но не дается колобок.

FOOTPRINTS IN THE SNOW

At sunset time across the fields
The young girls' footprints go
As from one village to the next
Their felt boots tramp the snow;

A child clings to its mother's breast;
Like lemon squash, sunlight
Flows into cavities and holes
To freeze like pools of light,

Or like the liquid white left when
An eggshell breaks in two:
Until the skis cut through its ice
With their long line of blue;

While, like a pancake into cream,
The moon glides sideways, fleet
As sleighs that run on in pursuit
But cannot catch this sweet.

ПОСЛЕ ВЬЮГИ

После угомонившейся вьюги
Наступает в округе покой.
Я прислушиваюсь на досуге
К голосам детворы за рекой.

Я наверно неправ, я ошибся,
Я ослеп, я лишился ума.
Белой женщиной мертвой из гипса
Наземь падает навзничь зима.

Небо сверху любуется лепкой
Мертвых, крепко придавленных век.
Все в снегу, двор и каждая щепка
И на дереве каждый побег.

Лед реки, переезд и платформа,
Лес и рельсы и насыпь и ров
Отлились в безупречные формы
Без неровностей и без углов.

Ночью, сном не успевши забыться,
В просветленьи вскочивши с софы,
Целый мир уложить на странице,
Уместиться в границах строфы.

Как изваяны пни и коряги
И кусты на речном берегу,
Море крыш возвести на бумаге,
Целый мир, целый город в снегу.

AFTER THE BLIZZARD

After the blizzard's cold rage has subsided
Over the scene a calm silence steals where
Idly I listen as over the river
Voices of children float through the still air.

Doubtless I'm wrong or mistaken or blind,
Doubtless demented: but whiter than death,
White as a woman who's fashioned of plaster,
Winter collapses upon the raw earth.

Dead, her shut eyelids lie under the sky
Which softly admires the pale form below;
Courtyards and forests are burdened with winter,
Twigs on the tree are each covered in snow.

Crossing and platform, ice on the river,
Forest and railway, are cast in design
Flawlessly modelled out of the darkness,
Measured to smoothness and perfect in line.

Night time, before the deep comfort of sleep,—
Oh, then inspired to leap up from bed,
Capture the whole world down, there on the page,
Limit its range to a verse's firm tread!

Thickets and stumps clearly sculptured to shape,
Riverside bushes, the rooftops' vast flow:
Only to bring them to life upon paper—
Snow, the whole world, whole town covered in snow!

ВАКХАНАЛИЯ

Город. Зимнее небо.
Тьма. Пролеты ворот.
У Бориса и Глеба
Свет, и служба идет.

Лбы молящихся, ризы
И старух шушуны
Свечек пламенем снизу
Слабо озарены.

А на улице вьюга
Все смешала в одно,
И пробиться друг к другу
Никому не дано.

В завываньи бурана
Потонули: тюрьма,
Экскаваторы, краны,
Новостройки, дома,

Клочья репертуара
На афишном столбе
И деревья бульвара
В серебристой резьбе.

И великой эпохи
След на каждом шагу —
В толчее, в суматохе,
В метках шин на снегу;

BACCHANALIA

A town. The winter sky.
The dark. A span of gates.
In Boris and Gleb Church
A service drones; and lights.

Devout brows, chasubles,
Old women's coats pulled tight,
All dimly shadowed by
The burning candlelight.

Outside in the street
The blizzards whirl and blow;
Men struggle yet can't reach
Each other through the snow.

Within the howling storm
The prison drowns from sight,
And excavators, cranes,
Homes and building site,

Some programme fragments stuck
Upon a hoarding, trees
Along the boulevard
Within a silver frieze.

Signs of a great era
Haunt every step you go:
The turmoil and the crush,
The tyre-marks in the snow,

В ломке взглядов — симптомах
Вековых перемен,
В наших добрых знакомых,
В тучах мачт и антенн;

На фасадах, в костюмах,
В простоте без прикрас,
В разговорах и думах,
Умиляющих нас.

И в значенье двояком
Жизни, бедной на взгляд,
Но великой под знаком
Понесенных утрат.

*   *   *

«Зимы», «Зисы» и «Татры»,
Сдвинув полосы фар,
Подъезжают к театру
И слепят тротуар.

Затерявшись в метели,
Перекупщики мест
Осаждают без цели
Театральный подъезд.

Все идут вереницей,
Как сквозь строй алебард,
Торопясь протесниться
На Марию Стюарт.

Молодежь по записке
Добывает билет
И великой артистке
Шлет горячий привет.

*   *   *

And broken viewpoints (signs
Of enduring changes),
The kindness of our friends,
Masts and aerial ranges,

Façades, and suits of clothes,
Natural simplicity,
And conversation, thoughts
That touch us movingly,

The double meaning of
A life that may seem shorn
But marks its greatness by
The losses it has borne.

*   *   *

Zisses, Zims and Tatras
That sweep up through the night
To theatres, dip lamps
And drown the road in light.

But lost out in the storm
As they sell theatre seats
Before the entrance, spivs
Keep wandering the streets,

While, filing through as though
Halberdiers lined the ways,
The crowd keeps struggling in
Where *Mary Stuart* plays.

Teenagers bringing chits
Are given special seats,
And give a fervent welcome
To greet the great artiste.

*   *   *

185

За дверьми еще драка,
А уж средь темноты
Вырастают из мрака
Декораций холсты.

Словно выбежав с танцев
И покинув их круг,
Королева шотландцев
Появляется вдруг.

Всё в ней жизнь, всё свобода
И в груди колотье,
И тюремные своды
Не сломили ее.

Стрекозою такою
Родила ее мать
Ранить сердце мужское,
Женской лаской пленять.

И за это, быть может,
Как огонь, горяча,
Дочка голову сложит
Под рукой палача.

В юбке пепельно-сизой
Села с краю за стол.
Рампа яркая снизу
Льет ей свет на подол.

Нипочем вертихвостке
Похождений угар,
И стихи, и подмостки,
И Париж, и Ронсар.

And there's a crush backstage
Where in the darkened room
The canvas scenery
Comes sprouting from the gloom.

Then, as a dancer breaks
Out from the circle's spree,
The Queen of Scots herself
Appears quite suddenly.

In her all's freedom, life,
Though in her breast lies pain:
But darkest prison vaults
Have weighed on her in vain.

This was the dragon-fly
Borne by her mother's womb
To wound the heart of man
And snare it with her charm;

And for this cause, perhaps,
Like fire, a flaming brand,
The daughter's head shall bow
Beneath the headsman's hand.

There in her ash-grey dress
She sat down in a chair:
Below, the bright footlights
Poured light upon her hair.

What does this coquette care
For ventures to afar,
The stage or poetry,
Or Paris, or Ronsard?

К смерти приговоренной
Что ей пища и кров,
Рвы, форты, бастионы,
Пламя рефлекторов?

Но конец героини
До скончанья времен
Будет славой отныне
И молвой окружен.

*   *   *

То же бешенство риска,
Та же радость и боль
Слили роль и артистку
И артистку и роль.

Словно буйство премьерши
Через столько веков
Помогает умершей
Убежать из оков.

Сколько надо отваги,
Чтоб играть на века,
Как играют овраги,
Как играет река,

Как играют алмазы,
Как играет вино,
Как играть без отказа
Иногда суждено,

Как игралось подростку
На народе простом
В белом платье в полоску
И с косою жгутом.

*   *   *

And now she's doomed to die,
What matter food or home?
Forts, bastions and moats,
And the reflector's flame?

For, her heroic death
Shall be, till all time ends,
Surrounded by high fame
And glory that transcends.

*　　*　　*

It is the same mad daring
And joy and pain that start,
That fuse the part and artist,
The artist and her part;

As though the chief rôle's passion
Could traverse all the years
And help a long-dead woman
To flee her torturers.

What courage do we need
To play for centuries
As all the valleys play
And as the river plays?

And as all jewels play,
And wine incessantly,
And one sometimes is doomed
To play on ceaselessly?

And as was played among
The people, by a girl
Whose white frock flowed with stripes,
Her plaited hair awhirl?

*　　*　　*

И опять мы в метели,
А она всё метет,
И в церковном приделе
Свет, и служба идет.

Где-то зимнее небо,
Проходные дворы,
И окно ширпотреба
Под горой мишуры.

Где-то пир.   Где-то пьянка,
Именинный кутеж.
Мехом вверх, наизнанку
Свален ворох одеж.

Двери с лестницы в сени,
Смех и мнений обмен.
Три корзины сирени.
Ледяной цикламен.

По соседству в столовой
Зелень, горы икры,
В сервировке лиловой
Семга, сельди, сыры.

И хрустенье салфеток,
И приправ острота,
И вино всех расцветок,
И всех водок сорта.

И под говор стоустый
Люстра топит в лучах
Плечи, спины и бюсты
И сережки в ушах.

Once more we're in the storm;
The blizzard still blows on
And lights shine in the church:
The service still goes on.

Somewhere's a winter sky,
Somewhere are passage ways,
The window of the store
Beneath a tinselled haze.

Somewhere are feasts and drinks,
Somewhere a birthday spree;
Piled furs, turned inside out,
Lie sprawled haphazardly.

The stair doors to the hall
Bring laughter, chatting men,
And three baskets of lilac
With icy cyclamen;

Laurels and caviare
Are in the room next door
Where salmon, herring, cheese,
Spread out their lilac show:

Then comes the napkins' crackle,
The pungency of spice,
All grades of wine matured,
All vodkas to suffice.

As myriad voices chat,
The beams of chandeliers
Drown shoulders, backs and busts
And gleaming rings in ears.

И смертельней картечи
Эти линии рта,
Этих рук бессердечье,
Этих губ доброта.

*   *   *

И на эти-то дива
Глядя, как маниак,
Кто-то пьет молчаливо
До рассвета коньяк.

Уж над ним межеумки
Проливают слезу.
На шестнадцатой рюмке
Ни в одном он глазу.

За собою упрочив
Право зваться немым,
Он средь женщин находчив,
Средь мужчин — нелюдим.

В третий раз разведенец
И дожив до седин,
Жизнь своих современниц
Оправдал он один.

Дар подруг и товарок
Он пустил в оборот
И вернул им в подарок
Целый мир в свой черед.

Но для первой же юбки
Он порвет повода
И какие поступки
Совершит он тогда!

*   *   *

But deadlier than grapeshot
Are such mouths that chat still,
These hands of heartlessness,
These lips full of goodwill.

*   *   *

And, gazing at these wonders
Like some strange maniac,
One man until the dawn
Drinks, silent, his cognac.

Upon him the unsettled
Lavish their sympathy;
But with his sixteenth glass
He's pure sobriety.

Assuring for himself
'Dumb' as a cognomen,
He's witty with the women,
Unsociable with men.

Divorced-thrice, now grey-haired,
He solely in his prime
Has justified the lives
Of women of his time;

The gifts of women friends
He put to circulation
And in return bestowed
All earth as his donation.

But, for the very first girl
He'll snap restraint in two,
And oh what startling deeds
Will he then surely do!

*   *   *

Средь гостей танцовщица
Помирает с тоски.
Он с ней рядом садится,
Это ведь — двойники.

Эта тоже открыто
Может лечь на ура
Королевой без свиты
Под удар топора.

И свою королеву
Он на лестничный ход
От печей перегрева
Освежиться ведет.

Хорошо хризантеме
Стыть на стуже в цвету.
Но назад уже время
В духоту, в тесноту.

С табаком в чайных чашках
Весь в окурках буфет.
Стол в конфетных бумажках.
Наступает рассвет.

И своей балерине,
Перетянутой так,
Точно стан на пружине,
Он шнурует башмак.

Между ними особый
Распорядок с утра,
И теперь они оба
Точно брат и сестра.

A danseuse in the guests
Is almost bored to death:
He goes to sit by her—
They're like twins of one breath!

She too quite clearly can
Recline to cheers that greet
A queen beneath the axe,
A queen without a suite.

He takes his queen outside
Upon the winding stair
Away from burning stoves
Into the fresher air;

For this chrysanthemum
The cold air brings redress
But he must now return
To crowds and stuffiness.

Tobacco in the tea-cups,
Stubs covering the bar,
Sweet-papers on the tables . . .
And daybreak is not far.

To win his ballerina
All that he needs to do
Is, like a watch spring-mounting,
To bend and lace her shoe.

With dawn they find a close
Relation to each other
Till both of them become
As sister and as brother.

Перед нею в гостиной
Не встает он с колен.
На дела их картины
Смотрят строго со стен.

Впрочем что им, бесстыжим,
Жалость, совесть и страх
Пред живым чернокнижьем
В их горячих руках?

Море им по колено,
И в безумьи своем
Им дороже вселенной
Миг короткий вдвоем.

*   *   *

Цветы ночные утром спят.
Не прошибает их поливка,
Хоть выкати на них ушат.
В ушах у них два-три обрывка
Того, что тридцать раз подряд
Пел телефонный аппарат.
Так спят цветы садовых гряд
В плену своих ночных фантазий.
Они не помнят безобразья,
Творившегося час назад.

Состав земли не знает грязи.
Все очищает аромат,
Который льет без всякой связи
Десяток роз в стеклянной вазе.
Прошло ночное торжество.
Забыты шутки и проделки.
На кухне вымыты тарелки.
Никто не помнит ничего.

Before her in the room
He lingers on his knees,
While pictures from the wall
Frown down on deeds like these.

But what, to their abandon,
Is conscience, fear or shame,
Before the living magic
Of both their hands aflame?

Oblivious of all,
Their madness can still prize
One brief instant together
More than all worlds and skies.

*   *   *

The night flowers slumber in the dawn,
Their heads unbowed by watering
Though buckets should pour over them;
But only in their ears still ring
Spasmodic snatches telling that
The phone sounds for the thirtieth time;
And in their flower beds they sleep
Imprisoned by night fantasies
Till even recent misbehaviour
Has faded from their memories.

Earth's substance lies immaculate
As stray perfumes go wandering
From roses in a crystal vase
And purify, cleanse everything . . .
So pass the night festivities,
Forgotten jokes and anticking:
The crockery is washed and clean:
No one remembers anything.

197

III

LATER POEMS

ЗА ПОВОРОТОМ

Насторожившись, начеку
У входа в чащу,
Щебечет птичка на суку
Легко, маняще.

Она щебечет и поет
В преддверьи бора,
Как бы оберегая вход
В лесные норы.

Под нею сучья, бурелом,
Над нею тучи.
В лесном овраге за углом
Ключи и кручи.

Нагроможденьем пней, колод
Лежит валежник.
В воде и холоде болот
Цветет подснежник.

А птичка верит, как в зарок
В свои рулады,
И не пускает на порог
Кого не надо.

За поворотом, в глубине
Лесного лога
Готово будущее мне,
Верней залога.

Его уже не втянешь в спор
И не заластишь.
Оно распахнуто, как бор
Всё вглубь, всё настежь.

Март 1958

ROUND THE CORNER

Perched up on the alert before
The wooded thicket's door
A bird sits chirping on a twig
In gentle-voiced allure.

There at the entrance to the wood
It chirps and sings its airs
As though it meant to guard the gate
To hidden forest lairs.

Beneath it, wind-blown branches twist:
Above it, stormclouds blow:
And round the corner in the grove
The shaded fountains flow;

While, heaped together, wind-felled logs
Lie hidden in their bower
As in the cold and watery swamp
A snowdrop bursts in flower.

Yet still the bird trusts in its songs
As though they were a vow
And will not suffer entrance to
All those who trespass now.

There round the corner in the deep
Dark thicket's secrecy,
More trusty than the bird's true voice
My future waits for me.

It's not a point for argument,
To win on to your side:—
It's open, like the pinewood's heart,
It lies there open wide!
March 1958

ВСЕ СБЫЛОСЬ

Дороги превратились в кашу.
Я пробираюсь в стороне.
Я с глиной лед, как тесто, квашу,
Плетусь по жидкой размазне.

Крикливо пролетает сойка
Пустующим березняком.
Как неготовая постройка,
Он высится порожняком.

Я вижу сквозь его пролеты
Всю будущую жизнь насквозь.
Все до мельчайшей доли сотой
В ней оправдалось и сбылось.

Я в лес вхожу, и мне не к спеху.
Пластами оседает наст.
Как птице, мне ответит эхо
И целый мир дорогу даст.

Среди размокшего суглинка,
Где обнажился голый грунт,
Щебечет птичка под сурдинку
С пробелом в несколько секунд.

Как музыкальную шкатулку
Ее подслушивает лес,
Подхватывает голос гулко
И долго ждет, чтоб звук исчез.

Тогда я слышу, как верст за пять,
У дальних землемерных вех
Хрустят шаги, с деревьев капит
И шлепается снег со стрех.

Март 1958

EVERYTHING CAME TRUE

The roads have weathered into gruel
And I must turn aside and go
And plash along a different path
And through the paste-ice, soft as dough.

A jay flies screeching overhead
Into a birch grove's emptiness
That, like an uncompleted building,
Uprears itself in nakedness;

And through its archways I can see
My whole life's future course lie bare
For all its small particulars
Are outlined and perfected there.

The snow-crust lies in layers where
I walk the wood unhurriedly,
And echoes give me their reply:
The way ahead grows clear for me.

In patches on the soaking loam
The bare earth is uncovering
While now and then, as seconds pass,
A bird keeps softly twittering

Her music, like a music box,
Until the forest overhears,
Relays it through its hollow throat,
And waits, waits, till it disappears;

Then long I hear how mile on mile
To distant signposts sounds still flow
Of crackling footsteps, dripping trees,
And from the eaves the splash of snow.
March 1958

ПАХОТА

Что сталось с местностью всегдашней?
С земли и неба стерта грань.
Как клетки шашечницы, пашни
Раскинулись, куда ни глянь.

Пробороненные просторы
Так гладко улеглись вдали,
Как будто выровняли горы,
Или равнину подмели.

И в те же дни, единым духом
Деревья по краям борозд
Зазеленели первым пухом
И выпрямились во весь рост.

И ни соринки в новых кленах,
И в мире красок чище нет,
Чем цвет берез светлозеленых
И светлосерых пашен цвет.

Май 1958

PLOUGHING TIME

Where is the landscape we once knew?
The frontiers of earth and sky
Are gone, and fields like chessboard squares
Alone stretch further than the eye;

And these expanses, hewn and ploughed,
Lie spread so evenly out there
That you might think the mountains had been
Levelled, or the vale swept bare.

On just these days, in one clean breath
The trees that fringe the furrowed soil
Burst green into their early leaf
And stretch till their full heights uncoil.

For no specks mar the new-sprung maple
And nowhere are there hues so pure
As is the pale-green of the birch
Or as the ploughland's grey allure.

May 1958

ПОЕЗДКА

На всех парах несется поезд,
Колеса вертит паровоз,
И лес кругом смолист и хвоист,
И что то впереди еще есть,
И склон березами порос.

И путь бежит, столбы простерши,
И треплет кудри контролерши,
И воздух делается горше
От гари, легшей на откос.

Беснуются цилиндр и поршень,
Мелькают гайки шатуна,
И тенью проплывает коршун
Вдоль рельсового полотна.

Машина испускает вздохи
В дыму, как в шапке набекрень,
А лес, как при царе Горохе,
Как в предыдущие эпохи,
Не замечая суматохи,
Стоит и дремлет по сей день.

И где-то, где-то города
Вдали маячат, как бывало,
Куда по вечерам устало
Подвозят к старому вокзалу
Новоприбывших поезда.

Туда толпою пассажиры
Текут с вокзального двора,
Путейцы, сторожа, кассиры,
Проводники, кондуктора.

THE JOURNEY

The train is running at full steam,
Its wheels whirled in the engine's glow
While round it resin pine-woods teem,
And there is still some way to go,
And up the banks the birches stream.

The track flies past, the signposts flare,
The long curls of the driver spill,
And bitter grows the flying air
With burning, milder down the hill.

The cylinder, the piston roars,
The nuts upon the steel rod shine,
As through the darkness a kite soars
Along the stretch of railway line.

And heavily it sighs out far
In smoke that marks its disarray,
But still, as when some fabled Tsar
Knew it in epochs passed away,
The wood ignores the wild furore
And stands and dreams up to this day.

And somewhere, somewhere, towns still loom,
As once they used to, distantly,
And there each evening wearily
To the old station endlessly
Trains with their new-arrivals come.

The heavy crowd of passengers
Goes streaming through the station yards
With guides and clerks and engineers
And with conductors and with guards.

Вот он со скрытностью сугубой
Ушел за улицы изгиб,
Вздымая каменные кубы
Лежащих друг на друге глыб.
Афиши, ниши, крыши, трубы,
Гостиницы, театры, клубы,
Бульвары, скверы, купы лип,
Дворы, ворота, номера,
Подъезды, лестницы, квартиры,
Где всех страстей идет игра
Во имя переделки мира.

Июль 1958

But, in ambiguous reticence,
The train steams past the curving street
And bellows smoke across these stones
Laid on each other, blocks complete
With posters, corners, pipes and roofs,
Lindens and squares and boulevards,
Hotels and theatres and clubs,
Astride with rooms and gates and yards,
Porches and stairs and flats upcurled
In which all passions are enwhirled
In order to remake the world.

July 1958

ЖЕНЩИНЫ В ДЕТСТВЕ

В детстве, я как сейчас еще помню,
Высунешься, бывало, в окно,
В переулке, как в каменоломне,
Под деревьями в полдень темно.

Тротуар, мостовую, подвалы,
Церковь слева, ее купола
Тень двойных тополей покрывала
От начала стены до угла.

За калитку дорожки глухие
Уводили в запущенный сад,
И присутствие женской стихии
Облекало загадкой уклад.

Рядом к девочкам кучи знакомых
Заходили, и толпы подруг,
И цветущие кисти черемух
Мыли листьями рамы фрамуг.

Или взрослые женщины в гневе,
Разругавшись без обиняков,
Вырастали в дверях, как деревья
По краям городских цветников.

Приходилось, насупившись букой,
Щебет женщин сносить, словно бич,
Чтоб впоследствии страсть, как науку,
Обожанье, как подвиг, постичь.

Всем им, вскользь промелькнувшим где-либо
И пропавшим на том берегу,
Всем им, мимо прошедшим, — спасибо,
Перед ними я всеми в долгу.

Июль 1958

WOMEN OF CHILDHOOD

Those days of childhood I recall again,
How you would lean out of the window's space
Into an almost quarry-like dark lane
Beneath the trees where noonday shadows trace.

The pavement and the roadway and the cellars,
To left, the church and dome: upon them all
Lay lowering the shadow of twin poplars
Whose shade crept to the corner down the wall.

And through the gate the muffled paths would steal
Into the long neglected garden's green
Wherein somehow the presences of women
Would cast a strange enigma on the scene.

There were the girls and hosts of friends they knew
Who dropped in, all the crowds of girls that came;
But how the flashing clusters of bird-cherry
Would wash their leaves across each window-frame!

And grown-up women who were heatedly
Brawling together with all barriers down,
Would sprout up in the doorways, just like trees
Along the edge of flower-beds in the town.

And then I sulkily had to endure
Lash-like the women prattling without end;
So loving them thereafter was a science,
Adoring them, a feat, to comprehend.

But to them all, who somewhere dimly gleam
And lose themselves upon that final shore,
To all as they fleet by, I give my thanks
And owe a debt I never can restore.
July 1958.

ПОСЛЕ ГРОЗЫ

Пронесшейся грозою полон воздух.
Все ожило, все дышит, как в раю.
Всем роспуском кистей лиловогроздых
Сирень вбирает свежести струю.

Все живо переменою погоды.
Дождь заливает кровель желоба,
Но все светлее неба переходы,
И высь за черной тучей голуба.

Рука художника еще всесильней
Со всех вещей смывает грязь и пыль.
Преображенней из его красильни
Выходят жизнь, действительность и быль.

Воспоминание о полувеке
Пронесшейся грозой уходит вспять.
Столетье вышло из его опеки.
Пора дорогу будущему дать.

Не потрясенья и перевороты
Для новой жизни очищают путь,
А откровенья, бури и щедроты
Души воспламененной чьей-нибудь.

Июль 1958

AFTER THE STORM

The air is heavy with the passing storm.
The world revives and breathes in paradise.
Through all the clusters of its blossoming
The lilac drinks freshness and vivifies;

And life pervades all in the weather's change
As over roofs the gutters flood their rain,
But brighter still grows heaven's distant range,
Higher beyond the dark clouds its blue chain.

Transcendent power lies in the artist's hand
That cleanses all things from impurity
And from his colour-bath newly transformed
Emerge the past, life, and reality.

Then memories of half a lifetime's age
Recede now with the passing of the storm:
This century outgrows its tutelage
To clear a way for all the years to come.

It is not some upheaval or uprising
Can lead us to the new life we desire—
But open truth and magnanimity
And the storm within a soul afire.

January 1958

ЗИМНИЕ ПРАЗДНИКИ

Будущего недостаточно,
Старого, нового мало.
Надо, чтоб елкою святочной
Вечность средь комнаты стала.

Чтобы хозяйка утыкала
Россыпью звезд ее платье.
Чтобы ко всем на каникулы
Съехались сестры и братья.

Сколько цепей ни примеривай,
Как ни возись с туалетом,
Все еще кажется дерево
Голым и полуодетым.

Вот, трубочиста замаранней,
Взбив свои волосы клубом,
Елка напыжилась барыней
В нескольких юбках раструбом.

Лица становятся каменней,
Дрожь пробегает по свечкам,
Струйки зажженного пламени
Губы сжимают сердечком.

* * *

Ночь до рассвета просижена.
Весь содрогаясь от храпа
Дом, точно утлая хижина,
Звякает дверцею шкапа.

WINTER FESTIVITIES

The future is not long enough,
The old and new are niggardly:
We need Eternity to stand
Among us like a Christmas tree;

We need the housewife to set out
A dress for her with stars in spray;
And each man's sisters, brothers, then
To come home for their holiday.

Yet though you try to hang up chains,
However much you fuss and care
In dressing her, the Christmas tree
Will still seem half-undressed and bare;

And see, though blacker than a sweep,
She still fluffs up her flowing hair
Into a bun, this proud madame
Who's dressed in several skirts that flare!

But, faces fall to stoniness,
And through the candles tremors start
As little darts of burning flame
Compress their lips to form a heart.

*   *   *

The house, that sat up all the night
Until the dawn, stirs from its snore
And rings, like some old ragged shack,
With each bang of the cupboard door.

Новые сумерки следуют,
День убавляется в росте.
Завтрак проспавши, обедают
Заночевавшие гости.

Солнце садится, и пьяницей
Издали, с целью прозрачной
Через оконницу тянется
К хлебу и рюмке коньячной.

Вот оно ткнулось, уродина,
В снег образиною пухлой
Цвета наливки смородинной,
Село, истлело, потухло.

Январь 1959

As day abbreviates its length
New twilights follow its retreat
While guests who slept on through the night
And through lunch-time, wake up to eat.

The sun sets, almost drunkenly,
As with intentions plainly read
He reaches through the window pane
Towards the cognac and the bread:

But see how this deformity
Has poked the snow with his plump snout
The colour of redcurrant vodka,
Sat down, and waned, and flickered out!

January 1959

НОБЕЛЕВСКАЯ ПРЕМИЯ

Я пропал, как зверь в загоне.
Где-то люди, воля, свет,
А за мною шум погони,
Мне наружу ходу нет.

Темный лес и берег пруда,
Ели сваленной бревно.
Путь отрезан отовсюду.
Будь что будет, все равно.

Что же сделал я за пакость,
Я убийца и злодей?
Я весь мир заставил плакать
Над красой земли моей.

Но и так, почти у гроба
Верю я, придет пора —
Силу подлости и злобы
Одолеет дух добра.

Январь 1959

THE NOBEL PRIZE

I've fallen beast-like in a snare:
Light, people, freedom, somewhere bide:
But at my back I hear the chase
And there is no escape outside.

Darkest wood and lakeside shore,
Gaunt trunk of a levelled tree,
My way is cut off on all sides:
Let what may, come; all's one to me.

Is there some ill I have committed?
Am I a murderer, miscreant?
For I have made the whole world weep
Over the beauty of my land.

But even at the very grave
I trust the time shall come to be
When over malice, over wrong,
The good will win its victory.

January 1959

БОЖИЙ МИР

Тени вечера во́лоса тоньше
За деревьями тянутся вдоль.
На дороге лесной почтальонша
Мне протягивает бандероль.

По кошачьим следам и по лисьим,
По кошачьим и лисьим следам
Возвращаюсь я с пачкою писем
В дом, где волю я радости дам.

Горы, страны, границы, озера,
Перешейки и материки,
Обсужденья, отчеты, обзоры,
Дети, юноши и старики.

Досточтимые письма мужские!
Нет меж вами такого письма,
Где свидетельства мысли сухие
Не выказывали бы ума!

Драгоценные женские письма!
Я ведь тоже упал с облаков.
Присягаю вам ныне и присно
Ваш я буду во веки веков.

Ну а вы, собиратели марок!
За один мимолетный прием
О какой бы достался подарок
Вам на бедственном месте моем!

Январь 1959

WIDE WORLD

As evening shadows finer-spun than hair
Streak out behind the trees and down the land
The postman comes along the forest path
To place a little package in my hand.

By paths that cats trace and where foxes go,
By paths where cats go and that foxes trace,
I bring the packet with my letters home:
There I shall give rein to my happiness!

For here are hills, lands, lakes and frontiers,
Here isthmuses and continents unfold:
And narratives, discussions, and reviews,
All children and young people and the old!

You masculine, inestimable letters!
Among you all there's not a single one
Containing stilted statements of dry thought
Or where some wit is not most plainly shewn!

You feminine, most treasurable letters!
Why, once *I* also made the clouds my clime!
I swear to you this moment and forever
I shall be yours until the end of time!

But as for you, oh all you stamp collectors,
How lucky would you not account your case
If for one brief and evanescent moment
You chanced to be in my unhappy place!

January 1959

ЕДИНСТВЕННЫЕ ДНИ

На протяженьи многих зим
Я помню дни солнцеворота,
И каждый был неповторим
И повторялся вновь без счету.

И целая их череда
Составилась мало-помалу —
Тех дней единственных, когда
Казалось нам, что время стало.

Я помню их наперечет:
Зима подходит к середине,
Дороги мокнут, с крыш течет,
И солнце греется на льдине.

И любящие, как во сне,
Друг к другу тянутся поспешней,
И на деревьях в вышине
Потеют от тепла скворешни.

И полусонным стрелкам лень
Ворочаться на циферблате,
И дольше века длится день,
И не кончается объятье.

Январь 1959

UNPARALLELED DAYS

Still through the range of many winters
I can recall those solstice days
With each day unrepeatable
Yet each repeated timeless ways;

And one by one their sequence grew
Together slowly to fulfil
Unparalleled those rare days when
It seemed to us that time stood still.

For I recount them one by one:
The winter halfway on its course,
Thaw on the roads, the dripping roofs,
The red sun warmer on thick ice;

Then lovers swiftly each to each
Are drawn, as in a dream they meet,
While cradled high up in the trees
The bird-cotes swelter in the heat;

The sleepy needle registers
Inertness on the dial's face,
And each day's longer than a lifetime,
And still unending each embrace.

January 1959

NOTES

The following notes pursue the limited aim of establishing for the reader not familiar with Pasternak's literary work as a whole the connexion between the individual poems and the principal trends underlying his other works, especially his prose writings. I have therefore, whenever possible, confined the notes to direct quotations from Pasternak's work. In a few cases I have allowed myself to comment on less familiar aspects of the Russian background to these poems. I have refrained from critical comment on the poems themselves and on the translation for different reasons: humble admiration as far as the poems are concerned, and profound sympathy for the sensitive and courageous translator in the gigantic difficulties he must have encountered in his task.

GEORGE KATKOV

I. THE POEMS OF YURY ZHIVAGO

The twenty-five poems which form the appendix to *Dr. Zhivago* are an essential part of the novel. They purport to be poems written by the hero and many of them allude to episodes in the novel. They have, however, an even closer relation to the life of Pasternak himself and to his spiritual development. They certainly represent the most mature and the most accomplished phase of his poetry. Ten of these poems were published, together with an announcement of the forthcoming appearance of the novel, in the literary magazine *Znamya* in Moscow in April 1954. They aroused great interest, the more so as no original poetry by Pasternak had been published since the end of the war, and created an atmosphere of expectation about the novel which was disappointed when it was rejected in 1956.

HAMLET (*page 3*)

The poem gives the key to the drama in which the publication of the novel was to be the crucial act. The poet tells us that he accepts his destiny as a human being in this unaccountable world. What momentarily gives him pause is the special part assigned to him, namely to be a witness to his time in the face of a hostile crowd. This drama is Pasternak's, not Zhivago's; Pasternak however, has tried to link this poem with the novel where it is referred to in Chapter 15. Zhivago has taken refuge from the world in the house where a few days later he was to be laid in his coffin. He spends his time revising his earlier poems and putting into writing his ideas on what the task of 'a new, truly modern art' should be. 'The seemingly incongruous and arbitrary jumble of things and ideas in the work of the symbolists (Blok, Verhaeren, Whitman) is not a stylistic fancy. This new juxtaposition of impressions is taken directly from life.' Zhivago then mentions his desire to write urbanistic poetry: 'The incessant rumbling by day and night in the street outside our walls is as much connected with our thoughts as the opening bars of an overture with the curtain, as yet dark and secret, but already beginning to crimson in the glow of the footlights. The incessant, uninterrupted rustle and movement of the town outside our doors and windows is a huge, immeasurable overture to life for each of us. It is in these terms that I should like to write about the town.' With these words the last note ever written by Zhivago ends. The author adds the following comment: 'There are no such poems in what has been preserved of Zhivago's work. Perhaps *Hamlet* belonged to such a series.'

The reference to the curtain beginning to glow before it goes up is significant; it is not reflected in the text of the poem but it establishes a connexion with an early prose fragment, published by Pasternak in 1918 and containing many elements later elaborated in *Dr. Zhivago*.*

The striking feature of the poem is the unexpected identification of Hamlet with Christ. Pasternak gives a clue to his meaning in an article published in 1956 in the almanach *Literaturnaya Moskva*. Here he writes, commenting on his translation of Shakespeare's *Hamlet*: 'Hamlet is not a drama of a weak character but a drama of duty and self-denial. When appearance and reality are seen to diverge and are separated by a gaping chasm it is of slight importance that the warning as to the world's falsity should come in a supernatural way and Hamlet be summoned to revenge by a ghost. It is of far greater importance that by the merest accident Hamlet should be chosen to sit in

* See Boris Pasternak, 'Without Love', in *Partisan Review*, 3–4, 1961, New York.

judgement on his time and become the servant of a remoter one. *Hamlet* is a drama of high vocation, of a call to heroic action in fulfilment of its hero's predestined task.' The self-denial of Hamlet, who gives up his position in the society into which he was born in order to 'do the will of Him that sent him' creates the poetic link with the Crucifixion and with Pasternak's own mission as he understood it.

The last line is a well-known Russian proverb, quoted *verbatim* and yet fitting faultlessly into the rhythm of the poem.

MARCH (*page 5*)

At first sight, this is a straightforward rhapsody of the return of life at the spring-tide. Might it not however conceal a secret meaning? The poem appeared first in *Znamya*, with a slight but significant variation in the last strophe. The reference to dung as the giver of life and the cause of growth, is omitted there and replaced by a commonplace poetical phrase. Could it be that Pasternak was alluding to other changes than those in the sequence of the seasons? Was there some allusion to an event in March 1953 which the cautious editor of *Znamya* thought perhaps sounded too daring?

IN HOLY WEEK (*page 7*)

In Holy Week, like *Earth* (number 21 of the Zhivago poems), is based on the comparison of the break of the seasons in early spring, with the liturgic sequence of the Holy Week services and their symbolic reference to human existence. This theme, which is later fully developed in *Mary Magdalen II* (poem 24 of the Zhivago series), is here only adumbrated. It is the abysmal despair of the days preceding the resurrection. The poem is full of allusions to the Holy Week services. The sleep of the earth is so deep that a supernatural effort is needed to overcome it. The chanting of psalms, mentioned in the first strophe, brings to mind the reading of the psalter which, according to Russian custom, goes on uninterruptedly for three days and nights at the side of the open coffin of a dead man. The church bells are silenced for the Holy Week (strophe 3) as in the Western Church. Christ's Passion (in the 4th strophe) refers to the service commonly known in the Orthodox Church as the Twelve Gospel Readings, that is, the vespers of Thursday night, during which twelve gospel accounts of Christ's passion are read. The congregation listens standing, and holding lighted candles. Note the contrast between the dignified behaviour of the trees in the country-side, and the undignified behaviour of those of the town parks. The Royal Gate (strophe 8) refers to the door in the screen dividing the altar from the choir and the congregation in an Orthodox Church. The scene is early morning service on Easter Saturday, when a procession carrying the Holy Shroud goes round the church. The reference to baked bread (strophe 9) is to the yeast bread used in the Orthodox Liturgy for the Host. Large quantities were baked near the churches on Good Friday in preparation for the Saturday and Sunday Mass. The poem ends in a tense atmosphere of expectation. The shrine from which March distributes his meagre alms to the beggars on the porch alludes possibly to the Ark of the Covenant of the Old Testament. The Acts of the Apostles, which are mentioned in the last but one strophe, refer to the lengthy reading period on the Saturday of Holy Week, preceding the Resurrection service (Easter Canon) which starts at midnight. The last strophe contains a promise that the sleepy vigil will end and the reference to the Resurrection (which will overcome death) is an allusion to the words in the Easter Hymn of the Orthodox Church: 'Christ has risen having vanquished death by death'.

WHITE NIGHT (*page* 13)

White Night is one of the poems with no direct bearing on the events described in the novel. The heroine, daughter of a minor landowner from southern Russia, was born in the town of Kursk, and has little similarity with the Lara of the novel. The poem introduces an important new character, the nightingale, which plays such a large part in the symbolism both of the novel and of the other poems. But here the nightingale—although a formidable singer—does not yet reveal the violent destructive side of his nature and is merely 'the lover of Primavera'.

SPRING FLOODS (*page* 17)

 The theme of the nightingale is developed in this poem in all its variations. The weary horseman riding to the solitary farm in the Urals reminds us of Zhivago on his last ride home, when he was stopped and captured by the partisans, except that Zhivago's ride must have happened later in the season. The double meaning of the word 'nightingale' is commented upon in the notes which Zhivago wrote during his first stay in the lonely house in Varykino. He noted in his diary: 'Chapter 7 of *Eugene Onegin* describes the spring, Onegin's house deserted in his absence, Lensky's grave by the stream at the foot of the hill.

> The nightingale, spring's lover
> Sings all night. The wild rose blooms.

Why "lover"? Well, it's a natural thing to say, it's fitting. "Lover" is right, and then he needed it for the rhyme with "the wild rose bush". But wasn't there also in his mind a sound image of "Nightingale the Robber", the character of the Russian epics?'

Zhivago goes on to quote from one of the epic ballads describing the legendary robber Nightingale who had his 'lair on seven oaks' and whose whistle could kill. According to some versions of the legend the robber Nightingale was vanquished and captured by the epic hero Ilya Muromets and later led a holy life in a Kiev monastery. The use of the same word to denote both a bird and a legendary robber serves to illuminate the contrast between the poetic and sublime character of love and its violent and even criminal side. At the same time the song of the nightingale, more than the song of any other bird, impressed Zhivago not only as expressing the triumphant fanfares of love, but also as a call for the awakening of the soul and for spiritual regeneration. '... once again,' Zhivago wrote in his diary, 'I wonder at the difference between the song of the nightingale and all other birds. . . . There were two phrases that stood out particularly. One was a luxurious, greedily repetitive "tiokh-tiokh-tiokh". At the sound of it the thicket, all covered with dew, shivered as though with pleasure. The other was grave, imploring, an appeal or a warning: "Wake up! Wake up!" '. In the poem the contrast becomes even more striking, the song rings 'like a tocsin' and the poet expects the singer to appear from the thickets in the shape of the robber Nightingale. The mention of the partisans brings us back to the narrative of the novel and the state of violent emotional confusion in which Zhivago found himself at the moment of his fateful capture by the partisan detachment.

THE WIND (*page 27*)

The love story of Zhivago develops far from the sea, under continental climatic conditions, but the imagery of the sea breaks into it with the strength of an obsession. In the poem *Parting* the poet expresses his own astonishment at these unaccountable analogies with the sea. 'And why does his mind surge with thoughts incessant of the sounding sea?' In *The Wind* this analogy is drawn most forcefully in the Russian, the link between the two images—the rhythmic waving of the pine trees in the forest and of the sailing boats at anchor in the bay—is possibly reinforced by the double meaning of the word 'kuzov', standing sometimes for the hull of a sailing boat, and sometimes for a wicker basket such as one takes to the forest when picking mushrooms.

INTOXICATION (*page* 29)

The poem is practically untranslatable, being entirely based on the equivocal meanings of the Russian word *khmel*, which is its title. *Khmel* means the hop plant and also the effect of an intoxicating drink—compare, for example, the expression 'to have *khmel* [hops] in the head', meaning to be drunk. The lovers are brought together in their search for cover from the storm. They think the tree under which they seek shelter is entwined with ivy, but discover that the plant which is growing on the tree is not ivy but hops, and their partnership, which begins as a search for safety, ends in a loving embrace.

INDIAN SUMMER (*page* 31)

The theme of this poem is the daily round of domestic life, seen to proceed in harmony with the changes of the seasons. This is also a theme in Zhivago's diary (see Chapter 10 of the novel). 'What happiness it is to work from dawn to dusk for your family and yourself, to build a roof over their heads, to till the soil to feed them, to create your own world like Robinson Crusoe, in imitation of the creator of the universe, and to bring forth your life, as if you were your own mother, again and again.'

The blackcurrent leaf mentioned in the first line of the poem would suggest to a Russian the season of pickling and salting cucumbers and mushrooms. Blackcurrant leaf was used widely as a herb for making brines.

THE WEDDING PARTY (*page* 33)

One of the gayest and most colourful poems of the series. The rhythm is that of the *chastushka*, the popular ribald factory song, often nonsensical, always mocking and usually accompanied on the accordion. The connexion with the *chastushka* style is established both by the mention of it in the 5th strophe and by the choice of words (for instance the accordion is referred to by the three different names under which it goes in Russia). As in the previous poem, a link between the revelling at the wedding, the course of nature and the significance of human life is established by introducing the image of the flight of pigeons.

Life is a kind of abandonment of oneself, a giving of oneself to others. The theme recurs in many poems of this cycle, especially in the last strophe of poem 19, *Daybreak*. 'Life is an abandonment like that of the revelling at a wedding, like that of a song, of a dream or of the flight of a grey-blue pigeon.' While welcoming the appearance of new poems by Pasternak in 1954, contemporary Soviet criticism did not agree with him on this last point. Life, according to one of these critics, was 'the building of socialism' rather than the flight of a grey-blue pigeon.

AUTUMN (*page* 37)

The contrast between good and evil in love, treated symbolically in the comparison of the singing nightingale, and the robber Nightingale in poem 5, is directly brought out in this poem. There is nothing in the novel which would correspond to the situation described here, but in the early *Chapter from a novel*, published in the thirties, there is a similar situation or at least one leading to it. There the hero of the novel, who is also the narrator, is expecting the arrival of a beautiful stranger to the Urals, to whom he has let a cottage in the park of the estate where the hero and his family have taken refuge in 1917. But the Lara of the novel was also 'the blessing of the baneful way' of Zhivago, and this is how he thought of her on his fateful last ride from Yuryatin before he was captured by the partisans.

A FAIRY TALE (*page* 41)

This is one of the central poems linking the contents of the lyrical part of the novel with the prose narrative, and also with the life of Pasternak himself. The story of St. George, as it spread through the oral tradition of the 'Religious poems' (*dukhovnye stikhi*), sung by the Russian equivalent of minstrels, is a fusion of the Byzantine story of the martyrdom of St. George and the western version of the liberation of the 'maiden' from the dragon. This explains the mixed style of imagery, in which the Russian landscape combines with a somewhat westernized medieval style. The writing of the poem by Zhivago is described in one of the tensest and most telling passages of the novel, in Chapter 14.

'Last night he had tried to convey, by means so simple as to be almost faltering and bordering on the intimacy of a lullaby, his feeling of mingled love and anguish, fear and courage, in such a way that it should speak for itself, almost independently of the words.

'Looking over these rough sketches now, he found that they needed a connecting theme to give unity to the lines, which were incoherent for lack of it. He crossed out what he had written and began to write down the legend of St. George and the Dragon in the same lyrical form. He started with a broad, spacious pentameter, but its harmony, derived from the metre itself and independent of the sense, annoyed him by its slick, humdrum sing-song. He gave up the pompous rhythm and the caesura and cut down the lines to four beats, as you cut out useless words in prose. The task was now more difficult but more attractive. The writing was livelier but still too verbose. He forced himself to still shorter lines. Now the words were crammed in a three-foot metre, and Yury felt wide awake, roused, excited; the right words to fill the short lines came, prompted by the measure. Things hardly named assumed form by suggestion. He heard the horses' hoofs ringing on the surface of the poem as you hear the canter of a horse in one of Chopin's Ballades. St. George was galloping over the boundless spaces of the steppe. He could watch him growing smaller in the distance. He wrote in a feverish hurry, scarcely able to keep up with the words as they poured out, always to the point and of themselves tumbling into place.'

In the novel, Zhivago is interrupted in his determined attempt to express his feeling 'of mingled love and anguish, fear and courage' by Lara who wakes up in fright, having heard the wolves howling on the other side of the ravine on which stands the forlorn house where they have taken refuge. 'She seemed very thin in her long nightdress and taller than she really was.

He started with surprise when she stood beside him, pale, frightened, stretching out her hand and whispering: "Do you hear a dog howling? . . . Oh, how terrible, it's a very bad omen" '. Even Lara at that moment looked like one of those figures in the medieval miniature illustrations of the St. George legend, also known in Russian iconography.

It would, however, be a mistake to identify the Lara of the novel with the woman who inspired her creator, and to whom the poems and quite especially the 'Fairy Tale' are dedicated. In the same Chapter of the novel Pasternak describes the process of Zhivago's work on the poems which he wrote out after his separation from Lara.

'He drank vodka and he wrote about Lara, but the more he crossed out and rewrote what he had written, the more did the Lara of his poems and notebooks grow away from her living prototype, from the Lara who was Katya's mother, the Lara who was away on a journey with her daughter.

'The reason for this correcting and rewriting was his search for strength and exactness of expression, but it also corresponded to the promptings of an inward reticence which forbade him to expose his personal experiences and the real events in his past with too much freedom, lest he should offend or wound those who had directly taken part in them. As a result, the steaming heat of reality was driven out of his poems and so far from their becoming morbid and devitalized, there appeared in them a broad peace of reconciliation which lifted the particular to the level of the universal and accessible to all. This was not a goal which he was consciously striving for; it came of its own accord as a consolation, like a message sent to him by Lara from her travels, like a distant greeting from her, like her image in a dream or the touch of her hand on his forehead, and he rejoiced at this ennobling of his verse.'

The relation of the poetic work to the 'steaming heat' of the real personal experience is doubtless the same as between the novel as a whole (including the poems) and the suffering and tribulations of Pasternak's own life.

AUGUST (*page* 49)

The poem has no relation to any episode in the novel, but is full of cryptic and mysterious significance. The poet recalls a dream which he obviously, for some reason, believes to be prophetic. He saw a procession of his friends going through a familiar landscape near Moscow in early autumn. They were gathering at his grave and there he seemed to hear his own voice forecasting the future and saying farewell to the woman he loved and who had become 'the battlefield' of his life's struggle. He takes leave of her knowing that for his sake she is challenging an 'abyss of humiliations', and while her struggle is going on he renounces all creative work and promises to remain silent. The situation to which Pasternak refers here, may well be that in which he found himself after the arrest of his friend and collaborator, Olga Ivinskaya, in 1948. There is more to it than that however; the mood in which the poem is written is not only one of acute grief at the loss which the poet suffered, but also of foreboding of a new tragedy. In this respect it is remarkable that the vision would be dated the 6th of August old style, the day of the Transfiguration of Our Lord. It was on that day, not quite three months after the death of Pasternak, that Olga Ivinskaya was arrested for the second time by the state police and once again had to face the challenge of 'an abyss of humiliations'.

WINTER NIGHT (*page* 53)

There is a direct reference to the poem in Chapter 3 of the novel. Yury Zhivago and his bride are driving in a cab to a Christmas party through the blizzard-swept streets of Moscow. 'As they drove through Kamerger Street, Yury noticed that a candle had melted a patch in the icy crust on one of the windows. Its light seemed to fall into the street as deliberately as a glance, as if the flame were keeping a watch on the passing carriages and waiting for someone.

' "A candle burned on the table, a candle burned . . ." he whispered to himself—the confused, formless beginning of a poem; he hoped that it would take shape of itself, but nothing more came to him.'

The candle which Zhivago had casually observed was burning in the room where Lara—unknown to him at that time—was meeting her future husband, a few moments before joining the Christmas party to which Zhivago and his bride were also going, and at which she would attempt to shoot her seducer Komarovsky. By a coincidence of which the symbolic significance has escaped some critics of *Dr. Zhivago*, it was in this very room that Zhivago lay in his coffin some fifteen years later, when Lara returned to

Moscow and found him. The poem, which Zhivago could not complete at the time, must have been written by him considerably later. It is certainly one of the most powerful of Pasternak's poetical works, and possibly of Russian lyrics in general. There is one circumstance which is puzzling, however. Such parties were held in Russia between Christmas day and the 7th of January. They might have been extended a few days beyond that date, but certainly no Christmas parties were given in February; yet the poem mentions that all through February the snow swept 'while on the table the candle stood burning'. What has February to do with the glimpse of the candle in the window of a house in the Kamerger Street? It is possible that by letting Zhivago postpone the completion of the poem to a much later date Pasternak wanted in a sense to give him an opportunity to relate the seemingly trivial episodes of his life to the great historical events that served as a background to it. The February in the poem might well be the February of 1917; it is noteworthy that the late Emperor Nicholas II, who recorded with almost morbid accuracy meteorological events in his diary (while omitting all reference to most of the political ones), had several times noted in his entries the blizzards which raged in February 1917.

PARTING (*page* 57)

Parting reflects the mood and the atmosphere of the novel during the period when Zhivago was living in Varykino after Lara's departure, slowly going out of his mind, turning nights into days and putting into poetry the story of their love and separation. As he did so 'the steaming heat of reality was driven out of his poems and so far from their becoming morbid and de-vitalized, there appeared in them a broad peace of reconciliation which lifted the particular to the level of the universal and accessible to all'. Zhivago 'rejoiced at this ennobling of his verse'. Besides this striving for the universal there are in *Parting* important details which refer to a very different situation from that of the separation from Lara in the novel. There is in the poem an element of surprise of a man who arrives at the home of the woman he loves, and finds she has gone. In *Zhivago* there was no such surprise. Zhivago knew in advance of Lara's departure and connived with Komarovsky in arranging it. Pasternak told his friends that the poem *Parting* was a

234

description of his own feelings when he learned of the first arrest of Ivinskaya in 1948. We can assume that the details are more those of the story of his own love than that of his hero Zhivago. Yet the relationships in the novel and in real life are substantially identical, the closeness and intimacy being in each case compared with the shifting line dividing the waves from the seashore.

> As, after storms, the surge flows up
> And covers reeds within its deep,
> So all her features drown in him:
> Their hidden image he will keep.

Commentators will speculate endlessly on the symbolical connexion between water and Lara; we should recall here only one sentence from Chapter 9, para 16, where Zhivago thinks of his future meeting with Lara: 'The promise of her nearness, cold as a white northern night . . . would reach him like the first wave of the sea as you run down over the sandy beach in the dark'. And in both cases it is the storm which rocked their lives, the 'unthinkable' circumstances of their existence that brought the lovers together, and not the search for romance of a lonely heart. *Znamya* published this poem without alterations in 1954. Few Soviet people can have failed to appreciate the situation described or to have recognized the reference to an unexpected arrest and the disorder of the room after a police search.

MEETING (*page* 61)

Znamya published the text of this poem without the last strophe and with small variations in the 4th strophe. Like other poems in the cycle, *Meeting* has a closer relation to Pasternak's own real life than to the events of the novel. The meeting is an imaginary one; the poet is meeting an image which is engraved 'by an iron chisel dipped in antimony' in his heart. It is this humble vision which makes the union of the lovers possible in spite of the 'mercilessness of the world' which has separated them, and this accounts for the mysterious last strophe (omitted in the *Znamya* text) which speaks of the non-existence of the lovers.

THE CHRISTMAS STAR (*page* 65)

In Chapter 3, para. 10 of the novel, young Yury Zhivago is

said to have promised an article on Alexander Blok—the symbolist poet—to his friend Gordon who was editing a stencilled undergraduate magazine. As Zhivago was driving with his future bride Tonya through the wintry streets of Moscow, it suddenly occurred to him: ' . . . that Alexander Blok was a manifestation of Christmas in the life and art of modern Russia—Christmas in the life of this northern city, Christmas underneath the starry skies of its modern streets and round the lighted trees in its twentieth-century drawing rooms. There was no need, so Zhivago thought, to write an article on Blok; all you needed do was to paint a Russian version of a Dutch "Adoration of the Magi" with snow in it, and wolves and a dark fir forest.' The poem is a fulfilment of this vision. The connexion with Blok is significant; it is surprising that Blok, who once said that Christ did not mean anything to him should, through his use of symbols as a method of understanding and interpreting reality, become a lode-star in Pasternak's approach to an understanding of Christianity.

DAYBREAK (*page* 73)

The 'you' whom the poet addresses in the first line is, according to Pasternak's own words, Christ. The poem relates to the last years of Zhivago's life during the period when he shared his room with the peasant painter Vasya. It is then, we are told, that he published a number of pamphlets which contained 'Yury's philosophy of life . . . , thoughts about religion and history (which had much in common with those of his uncle and of Sima) as well as his poems'. (*Dr Zhivago*, Chapter 15, para. 5.) The views of Sima referred to, can be found in the novel, Chapter 13, para. 17. They are a naïve interpretation of the symbolism of the Old and New Testaments, which is at the same time an interpretation of life and of the human condition. Looking at the poem in connexion with Pasternak's own life, *Daybreak* appears to be of even greater significance; it refers to that peculiar conversion to which, it is reported, he alluded when he described his religious convictions as those of 'an atheist who has lost his faith'. This conversion which—like that of Zhivago—is only hinted at in the novel, was hardly a change of metaphysical convictions or an acceptance of a new moral code based on the Gospels. Pasternak's conversion was primarily a total change of his poetic vision. For him the acceptance of the New Testament, which was like an

awakening or a coming to life after a swoon, was the acceptance of
the story and legend of Christianity as a system of symbols which,
when applied to everyday life, changes it beyond recognition. To
say this is not to deny but to affirm the fact of new religious
experience in the life of the poet. This illumination which came
over the poet in the first months of World War II, finds its
expression in the poem *Daybreak*, to which *The Christmas Star*
serves as an introduction. *The Christmas Star* points out and
extols the symbolical significance of the Nativity in the course
of the following centuries in all aspects of life: in art, in the day's
round, in children's folklore and in human contacts. In *Daybreak*
the import of the New Testament as a whole for modern metro-
politan urban conditions is revealed. This is not merely a question
of aesthetic perception of modern life, it leads to a renewal of
interhuman relations, a renewal which Pasternak describes
paradoxically—after admitting that he would like to 'put everybody on their knees'—when he says that his only victory is to be
conquered by his fellow beings.

Daybreak is an introduction to a sequence of poems directly
inspired by a reading of the Gospels and of liturgical texts from
the Holy Week services of the Eastern Church.

THE MIRACLE (*page* 77)

The Miracle is a further illustration of how the Gospel story,
when absorbed by the creative imagination of the poet, alters
our perception of the course of nature. Pasternak seems to think
that belief in the miracles of the New Testament differs from
belief in magic, because the miracle in Christian interpretation
is a revelation of God's providence which occurs, not at the
moments of our strength, but at times when we are dismayed
and go astray. There can be no doubt that Pasternak believed his
own poetry to be 'miraculous' in that sense. See *August* where
he says farewell to his 'wonder-working might'.

EARTH (*page* 81)

By placing this poem in the sequence of the 'religious poems'
of Zhivago, Pasternak must have pursued a special purpose. The
poem draws the same parallel between the daily round and the
changes in nature which we have already met in other poems,

especially *Holy Week*. The comparison leads the poet to interpret the April dripping thaw as tears shed over the thousand tales of human misery known to nature but ignored by modern man. And the poet pledges himself to voice the lament he has overheard in the music of nature as it awakens in early spring. In the last strophe the allusion is certainly to the Last Supper: the poet finds in the Lenten services, particularly in those of Holy Week, inspiration in his task of ensuring 'that a hidden stream of suffering may warm the coldness of existence'. See also D. D. Obolensky's comments on this poem in an article which appeared in the *Review of Slavonic and East European Studies* in December 1961.

EVIL DAYS (*page* 85)

Evil Days, to an even greater extent than the preceding poem, suggests topical interpretations of the Gospel story. These interpretations are strengthened in the Russian text by the choice of contemporary and colloquial expressions side by side with the traditional words of the Gospel. However, any attempt to specify the function of Pasternak's symbols at this level of poetic abstraction would be ridiculous. The power of a symbolical representation of the world (whether in myth, legend, parable or modern symbolist poetry), resides in the capacity of the symbol for living a life not foreseen or intended by its creator. A symbol continues to live, have significance, and guide and illuminate humanity even when the historical circumstances in which it was originally conceived have altered; while performing a different symbolic function, it establishes a link between the changing patterns of reality.

MARY MAGDALEN (*page* 89)

In these two poems the poetical use of New Testament symbolism is at its most powerful. The theory of this poetic reconstruction is contained in the novel in Chapter 13, para. 17 —the conversation between Lara and Sima Tuntseva, an ecstatic provincial maiden who had, in the first years of the revolution, become a kind of lay preacher. Lara talks to Zhivago about Sima in the following words: 'They say Sima is a bit odd— not quite right in the head. It's true she doesn't seem quite normal but that's only because she is so deep in religion. You and she are extraordinarily alike in your views.' And having heard Sima's philosophizing, Zhivago comes to the conclusion that she borrowed freely from the writings of his uncle Kolya, the typical Russian lay theologian of the beginning of the century. 'But all the same' (says Zhivago) 'how intelligent she is and how gifted.'

Sima's rambling philosophical talk should be read in order to understand the full significance of the *Mary Magdalen* poems. She begins by commenting on certain liturgical texts of the Lenten services. 'A lot of liturgical texts bring together the concepts of the Old and the New Testaments and put them side by side. For instance, the burning bush, the exodus from Egypt, the children in the fiery furnace, Jonah and the whale, are compared to the virgin birth and the resurrection of Christ.

'These comparisons bring out, very strikingly, I think, the way in which the Old Testament is old and the New is new. Quite a lot of texts compare the virgin birth to the crossing of the Red Sea by the Jews. . . . What kind of events are they? Both are super-natural, both are equally recognized as miracles. But there is a difference between the two miracles—a difference in the kind of thing people thought of as miraculous in these two different periods, the one ancient and primitive, the other new, post-Roman, more advanced.

'In one case you have a national leader, the patriarch Moses, ordering the sea to withdraw, and at the stroke of his magic staff it parts and allows a whole nation—countless numbers, hundreds of thousands of people—to go through, and when the last man is across, it closes up again and submerges and drowns the pursuing Egyptians. The whole picture is in the ancient style—the elements obeying the magician, great jostling multitudes like Roman armies on the march, a people and a leader. Everything is visible, audible, deafening, tremendous.

'In the other case you have a girl—a very commonplace figure who would have gone unnoticed in the ancient world—quietly, secretly, bringing forth a child, bringing forth life, bringing forth the miracle of life, the 'life of all' as he was afterwards called. The birth of her child is not only illegitimate from the standpoint of the scribes, it is also against the laws of nature. She gives birth not of necessity but by a miracle, by an inspiration. And from now on, the basis of life is no longer to be compulsion, it is to be that very same inspiration—this is what the New Testament offers—the unusual instead of the commonplace, the festive instead of the workaday, inspiration instead of compulsion.

'You can see what an enormously significant change it is. Why should a private human event, completely unimportant if judged by ancient values, be compared to the migration of a whole people? Why should it have this value in the eyes of heaven? For it is through the eyes of heaven that it must be judged, it is before the face of heaven and in the sacred light of its own uniqueness that it all takes place.'

After a short digression containing a criticism of the mortification texts of the Lenten services ('I always think they were composed by fat monks who didn't keep their Rule!') Sima goes on to comment on a text of the Wednesday morning service in Holy Week which is a Slavonic translation of a Byzantine spiritual poet, the nun Kassia of the ninth century.

'It has always interested me that Mary Magdalen is mentioned on the very eve of Easter, on the threshold of the death and resurrection of Christ. I don't know the reason for it, but this reminder seems to me so timely at the moment of his taking leave of life and before he takes it up again. Now look at the way the reminder is made—what genuine passion there is in it and what a ruthless directness.

' "Unbind my debt, as I unbind my hair."—It means: "As I loosen my hair, do Thou release me from my guilt." Could any expression of repentance, of the thirst to be forgiven, be more concrete, more tangible?

'And later on in the liturgy of the same day there is another, more detailed passage, and this time it almost certainly refers to Mary Magdalen.

'Again she grieves in a terribly tangible way over her past and over the corruption which is rooted in her, so that every night it comes to life in her once more. "The flaring up of lust is to me like night, the dark, moonless zeal of sin." She begs Christ to accept her tears of repentance and be moved by the sincerity of her sighs, so that she may dry His most pure feet with her hair—reminding Him that in the rushing waves of her hair Eve took refuge when she was overcome with fear and shame in paradise. "Let me kiss Thy most pure feet and water them with my tears and dry them with the hair of my head, which covered Eve and sheltered her when, her ears filled with sound, she was afraid in the cool of the day in paradise." And immediately after all this about her hair, she exclaims: "Who can fathom the multitude of my sins and the depth of Thy judgement?" What familiarity, what equal terms between God and life, God and the individual, God and a woman!'

In the poems, however, the treatment of the liturgical texts is extremely free so that one can speak only of the presence of the spirit of Kassia's poem in Pasternak's variation of the Mary Magdalen theme.

GETHSEMANE (*page* 95)

In contrast to the treatment of the Mary Magdalen theme in the two preceding poems, *Gethsemane* closely follows the account of the Gospels and is remarkable for the way it brings together the many threads which connect it with the other poems of Zhivago, and with the philosophy of the novel. The most important connexion is, of course, *Hamlet* (see note to the first poem of the series). In *Gethsemane*, however, Pasternak takes a further step in the interpretation of the poet's mission in the world. In its development through the ages, humanity produces myths, legends and parables in which its hopes and aspirations find their symbolic expression. There are certain moments in history, however, when as Pasternak says in the second but last strophe, the march of the ages becomes overheated like the axle of a carriage, and bursts into flame. At such moments parables and myths coincide with reality, and the creative bearers of the ideas symbolically expressed in preceding ages are led by cruel and sublime necessity to make not a symbolical but a real sacrifice, as witnesses of their time and as doers of their Father's will. In this sense Pasternak interpreted his poetic mission as an apostolic one.

II. WHEN THE SKIES CLEAR

IT'S UNBECOMING (*page* 105)

In his autobiography* Pasternak touches on the same subject as in this poem when he recalls the loss of his own manuscripts and even of published works. Some of his books and manuscripts were destroyed in the house of the German family where

* *An Essay in Autobiography*, translated by Manya Harari. Collins and Harvill Press, London, 1957.

he was a private tutor during the anti-German demonstrations in Moscow in 1915. This recollection brings him to a general consideration of the loss of his earlier works.

'Later I lost many of my manuscripts in more peaceful circumstances. I dislike my style before 1940, just as I quarrel with half of Mayakovsky's writings and with some of Yesenin's. I dislike the disintegrating forms, the impoverished thought and the littered and uneven language of those days. I have no regrets for the faulty works I lost. For quite a different reason I do not regret the loss of my successful writings either.

'It is more important in life to lose than to acquire. Unless the seed dies it bears no fruit. One must live tirelessly, looking to the future, and drawing upon those reserves of life which are created not only by remembrance, but also by forgetting.

'At various times and for various reasons I have lost: my paper on *Symbolism and Immortality*, several articles written in my futuristic period, a fairy-tale for children in prose, two poems, a note-book of verse which should have come between *Above the Barriers* and *My Sister Life*, several foolscap notebooks containing the rough draft of a novel (except for the first chapter which I revised and published as a story, *The Childhood of Luvers*) and the translation of one whole tragedy from Swinburne's trilogy on Mary Stuart.'

MY SOUL (*page* 107)

The most tragic poem of the series, *My Soul* is a passionate assertion of the poet's solidarity with his innumerable friends who were either shot or imprisoned or driven by the circumstances of their lives to suicide in the last forty years of his life. The poem can be dated by the last strophe as having been written in 1955 or 1956. In his autobiography Pasternak devotes a chapter to a few of his friends who perished. Ilya Ehrenburg reacted to these pages by saying that he could not read them without a feeling of embarrassment. Well he might.

In spite of the note of almost unrelieved sadness, the poem is not a pessimistic one. The sufferings and death of his friends will not be in vain, the poet tells us, if only his soul can continue to assimilate them into a compost, the grave's compost which will nurture future growth. One is tempted to draw an analogy between this poetical figure and the meaning of the last strophe of *March*, from the poems of Zhivago.

THE CHANGE (*page* 113)

One of the few poems in which one seems to hear an echo of Mayakovsky's didactic denunciatory style. But how different is the 'lesson' conveyed by Pasternak. His acquaintance with low life in Moscow is documented in his early prose, especially in the fragment called in translation *The Last Summer* (translation by G. Reavey with introduction by Lydia Slater, published by Penguin Books). Yet the protest against the falseness of compulsory optimism (preached by those who consider the misfortunes of the human condition as a blemish and a shame) are common both to Mayakovsky and Pasternak. In the third strophe 'they granted' should be understood as meaning 'I was granted the honour' to be counted among the dregs of society.

MUSHROOMING (*page* 119)

Picking mushrooms was one of Pasternak's favourite hobbies. This activity differs from the picking of mushrooms in England. Mushrooms have been for centuries an essential part of peasant diet, and they include a large range of fungi, each with a well-known popular name, each with its own habits of growth and its own habitat in the forest. It was on these mushroom-picking walks through the forest that Pasternak discussed his novel with literary friends and read them his poems from it. Perhaps the ambience of picking mushrooms made him believe that he had been approved and understood by them. Later some of his fellow mushroom-pickers signed the document rejecting the publication of Pasternak's novel in the Soviet Union.

THE LINDEN AVENUE (*page* 125)

The linden or lime tree has a special significance in Pasternak's poetry. Compare the first poem of this series, where the poet plans to write 'eight lines on the properties of passion':

> And like a garden set my rhymes:
> Within it on the hour
> The trembling lindens row by row
> Would one by one break flower!

There must have been some special experience in the poet's life connected with the hot summer of 1917 which gave the smell of lime blossom unusual significance. *Dr. Zhivago*, Chapter 5, may perhaps give a clue to this almost obsessive preoccupation with lime blossom. On his way from the front to Moscow, Yury Zhivago becomes conscious of the scent of lime blossom as if it were a message or a memento to him: 'Then, like a message delivered on the way or like greetings from Melyuzeyevo, as though addressed personally to Yury, there drifted in the familiar aromatic smell. It came from somewhere to one side of the window and higher than the level of either garden or wild flowers, and it quietly asserted its excellence over all else. Kept from the windows by the crowd, Yury could not see the trees; but he imagined them growing somewhere very near and spreading over the carriage roof their tranquil branches covered with dusty leaves as thick as night and sprinkled with constellations of small, glittering wax flowers.

'Everywhere along the way there was the noisy crowd, and everywhere the lime trees were in blossom.

'Their scent seemed to be everywhere at once and to overtake the travellers on their journey north, like a rumour flying round each siding, signal-box and halfway-halt and waiting for them on arrival, established and confirmed.'

WHEN THE SKIES CLEAR (*page* 129)

When the Skies Clear was to be the title of the second part of the collection of verse which, together with the poems of Dr. Zhivago, was to appear under the general title of *In the Interlude*. Originally the sequence was to have had thirty-four poems, ending with *Bacchanalia*; the last poems added to the present series are dated after the publication of *Dr. Zhivago* abroad and the memorable events connected with the award of the Nobel Prize to Pasternak. The poet wanted them to be added to the collection *When the Skies Clear*. This poem, like all the rest in the series, was born of the atmosphere of relaxation and belated happiness which the poet enjoyed in his late sixties after his friend, Olga Ivinskaya, had been released in 1953 from her first spell in a concentration camp.

BREAD (*page* 131)

There is—as all too often elsewhere—an untranslatable element in this poem. *Khleb* means not only 'bread' in Russian but also, especially in the plural *khleba*, 'the standing corn'. This hymn to the sacred and sacramental significance of bread was published in 1955 in the Soviet literary magazine *Oktyabr*. The last line, however, appeared there in the variant 'and all its births, toil and deaths'.

THE AUTUMN WOOD (*page* 133)

It would probably be pedantic to interpret the roll-call of the cockerels resounding in the forest as a symbol or allegory of the relations between the poets of various epochs and various lands. And yet it is this kind of scarcely definable allusion to matters of a very different order (e.g., of a social, historical or metaphysical character) that endows Pasternak's nature descriptions with a charm and significance with which vulgar realism cannot compete. This applies equally to the subsequent nature poems of Pasternak.

FOUR FRAGMENTS ON BLOK (*page* 153)

Alexander Blok, whom Pasternak met only once in his life, shortly before his tragic and almost voluntary death in despair and desolation, early became and always remained one of the most powerful influences on Pasternak's poetry. He speaks of Blok in the third chapter of his autobiography hesitantly, as if fearing to fall into the triteness of literary criticism. 'Blok was part of my youth, as of the youth of others of my generation . . . He had all the qualities which go to make a great poet—passion, gentleness, dedicated insight, his own conception of the world, his own gift of transforming everything he touched, his own reserved, restrained, self-effacing destiny. Of all these qualities and many others besides, I will mention only one aspect—I found it the most striking and it therefore seemed to me predominant in him: his swiftness, his wandering yet attentive glance, the quickness of his observation.' See also the note on the poem *The Christmas Star*.

The second strophe of the first Fragment is a sarcastic reference to the pointless discussions on Pushkin's merits which went on in the twenties and early thirties between the various literary cliques in Soviet Russia. The reference to Blok at the end of the fragment is more serious. Astonishingly, Soviet literary criticism never made any serious attempt to dress up Blok as a 'representative' of something or other. His poetry was too much alive in the minds of all Pasternak's generation to make such attempts hopeful of success. The identification of Blok with the wind in the second Fragment is based on the meaning of the adjective *vetrenny* and the substantive *vetrenik* in Russian. Both suggest a light-headed, irresponsible or slightly unsettled person. The Jacobin grandfather is A. N. Beketov, who in his youth 'was a follower of Fourier and Saint-Simon, and belonged to the noble generation of Russian romantic idealists' (Mochulsky, *Alexander Blok*, YMCA Press, Paris, 1948). Blok grew up on his grandfather's estate Shakhmatovo, near Moscow, and the landscape of the central Russian wooded plain was an inspiration both for his poetry and that of Pasternak. It is the windswept element in Blok's poetry, its pervasive fluidity, that is dominant in the poems of Blok's maturest phase (published in the third volume of his collected poetic works, which appeared in his lifetime); especially is this true of *The Twelve*, a unique poetic vision of the revolutionary events of 1917, with which perhaps only *Dr. Zhivago* could be compared. In the third Fragment there is an allusion to an event in Blok's life which is anachronistically transferred in the poem to Blok's childhood. But the essence of the reminiscence is retained in the poem. Mochulsky, in his book on Blok, tells us that in the last year of his life Blok intended to write an autobiographical work, to be entitled *Neither Dreams nor Reality*. The first chapter was to be entitled 'How our peasants sang twenty years ago'; it opened with the following words:

'We were all, the entire family, sitting under the lime-trees at sunset, having tea. Behind the lilac bushes the mist was already rising from the gully . . . The peasants from the neighbouring village came out to cut the grass on the meadow belonging to a merchant. The scythes swished through the grass, and judging from the sound there must have been some twenty of them. All of a sudden one of the reapers started singing; his powerful silvery tenor flowed freely, flooding the gully and the wood and the garden. The peasants joined in the singing. And all of us grew terribly embarrassed . . . I did not know the words and could not distinguish them, and the song became louder and louder . . . I felt uneasy sitting there motionless, I felt a tickling in my throat, I was near bursting into tears. I got up suddenly and rushed into a distant corner of the garden.'

'From the moment this song was heard' (Mochulsky tells us) 'everything lapsed into chaos and confusion; the merchant took to drink and fired the hay-ricks on his estate; a political agitator made his appearance and could be seen cycling to and fro along the lanes. The peasants' huts fell into disrepair, and the peasants did nothing to mend them. And the author of the story, seized by an unaccountable lust for destruction, cut down the century-old lilac bushes and the adjoining birch wood.'

The last of the four Fragments on Blok deals with his lyrics of foreboding, of Blok's 'dread desire' for the storm which was to do away with the world in which he lived. This foreboding, as Pasternak tells us in the epilogue to the prose section of *Dr. Zhivago*, was still only figurative in Blok's day. Zhivago's friend Gordon makes the following observation some time in 1943 while serving at the front: 'Take that line of Blok's, "We, the children of Russia's terrible years": you can see the difference of period at once. In his time, when he said it, he meant it figuratively, metaphorically. The children were not children, but the sons, the heirs of the intelligentsia, and the terrors were not terrible but apocalyptic; that's quite different. Now the figurative has become literal, children are children and terrors are terrible. There you have the difference.' The revolution was one of those moments of history when the march of ages bursts into flame (see note on *Gethsemane*). The allegorical visions of Blok merged into dire reality. The mission of the poet in Blok's day had been prophecy; in Pasternak's it became one of apostolic service.

IN HOSPITAL (*page* 163)

In 1952 Pasternak was struck down by a severe heart attack and was taken to hospital, where he had to stay for a considerable time. The image in the last strophe might well go back to some recollection of Rilke, whom Pasternak knew personally and whose poems he translated into magnificent Russian verse.

MUSIC (*page* 167)

On Pasternak's attitude to music see his *An Essay in Autobiography*, Chapter 2—Skryabin, and also his article on Chopin published in Russian in 1946 and in an English translation in the *Manchester Guardian.*

AFTER THE INTERLUDE (*page* 171)

This poem, introducing four magnificent winter poems contains perhaps the first premonition of the poet's approaching death.

BACCHANALIA (*page* 183)

The longest poem and the last of the original series *When the Skies Clear* is different in style and content from all the other poems. The autobiographical references (Pasternak translated Schiller's *Maria Stuart*, which became a regular feature of the repertoire of the Maly Teatr) are unmistakable. The attitude of the poet to the great epoch in which he lives is partly satirical, partly serious. Perhaps what he says in Zhivago's words at the end of the novel gives a clue to the author's intentions. Writing of the poetry of the symbolists (see note on *Hamlet*) Zhivago notes shortly before his death:

'Just as they hurry their succession of images through the lines of their poems, so the street in a busy town hurries past us with its crowds and its broughams and carriages at the end of the last century, or its trams, buses and electric trains at the beginning of ours.

'Where, in such a life, is pastoral simplicity in art to come from? When it is attempted, its pseudo-artlessness is a literary fraud, not inspired by the countryside but taken from academic book-shelves. The living language of our time is urban.

'I live over a busy crossing. Moscow, blinded by the sun and the white heat of her asphalt yards, scattering sun gleams from her top floor windows, breathing and blossoming with the colour of her streets and clouds, is whirling all round me, turning my head and willing me to turn the heads of others by writing in her praise.

'The incessant rumbling by day and night in the street outside our walls is as much connected with our thoughts as the opening bars of an overture with the curtain, as yet dark and secret, but already beginning to crimson in the glow of the footlights. The incessant, uninterrupted rustle and movement of the town outside our doors and windows is a huge, immeasurable overture to life for each of us. It is in these terms that I should like to write about the town.'

248

III. LATER POEMS

ROUND THE CORNER (*page* 201)

This and the following eight poems were written in the period succeeding the publication of *Dr. Zhivago*, its condemnation in the Soviet Union, the award of the Nobel Prize to Pasternak and his refusal to accept it. Most of these poems are topical, and are a record of the tremendous nervous tension and mental strain under which Pasternak had to live out the last months of his life. *Round the Corner* takes up the theme, familiar to us from a number of poems in *Dr. Zhivago*, of a bird singing in a thicket in some distant forest. The identification of the poet and the bird is now expressly admitted. The premonitions first expressed in *Hamlet* are also taking more definite shape. The future, which is now beyond doubt and argument, is both the triumph of the poet's mission and the imminent end of his earthly existence.

THE JOURNEY (*page* 207)

A late return to the urban style of which Zhivago was dreaming in the notes written shortly before his death. Note the crowding of substantives in the description of the modern city, which is here contrasted with the country, where nothing has changed from time immemorial. In order to understand the changes occurring in the life of the city and to appreciate the use of the substantives in the description of the townscape the reader should compare this poem with the description of Moscow in strophe 38 of Chapter 7 of Pushkin's *Eugene Onegin*.

WOMEN OF CHILDHOOD (*page* 211)

Compare *An Essay in Autobiography*, page 30, where Pasternak speaks of his childhood. 'Our neighbourhood was extremely sordid; it was close to the Tverskiye-Yamskiye, the Pipe and the lanes of Tsvetnoy. You were always being dragged away; you were not supposed to hear this, you were not allowed to know that. But sometimes nannies and wet-nurses wearied of isolation, and then we were surrounded by all sorts of company.

'And at noon the mounted police drilled on the parade ground of the Znamensky Barracks.

'As a result of all this rubbing shoulders with beggars and pilgrims, and of nearness to the world of the rejected and of listening to their stories of troubles and hysterics I was filled too early, and for life, with a compassion for women, so terrible that it was hardly to be borne, and with a still more anguished pity for my parents who would die before me and whom it was my duty to deliver from the pains of hell by some shining deed, unheard-of and unique.'

AFTER THE STORM (*page* 213)

Written just before the Nobel Prize crisis, this poem is like an echo of Pushkin's *Last Cloud of the Receding Storm*. The last strophe is a final answer in aphoristic form to those who tried to insinuate that Pasternak was guilty of advocating a change in Russia's political life by means of 'upheaval or insurrection'.

WINTER FESTIVITIES (*page* 215)

There is little of the optimism of *After the Storm* in this, one of the last poems of Pasternak known to us. A profound sense of disappointment with the circumstances of his private life seems to constitute the background of the poem. Neither the faithful observance of a bygone tradition nor hope for the future can make sense of the Christmas celebrations. 'We need Eternity to stand among us like a Christmas tree'. Here again there is possibly a premonition of the poet's imminent death.